S0-AFZ-860

EXTRAORDINARY LIVING

To: Derek

In service,

EXTRAORDINARY LIVING

The Hidden Power That Answers
Life's Most Compelling Question

D O N A L D   C L I N E B E L L

PUBLISHING & MARKETING
Oviedo, Florida

Extraordinary Living: The Hidden Power That Answers Life's Most Compelling Question by Donald Clinebell

Published by

HigherLife Publishing & Marketing, Inc.

PO Box 623307

Oviedo, Florida 32765

www.ahigherlife.com

This book or parts thereof may not be reproduced in any form, stored in a retrieval system, or transmitted in any form by any means—electronic, mechanical, photocopy, recording, or otherwise—without prior written permission of the publisher, except as provided by United States of America copyright law.

Copyright © 2016 by Donald Clinebell. All rights reserved.

Paperback ISBN: 978-1-939183-87-3

ebook ISBN: 978-1-939183-88-0

Cover Design: David Whitlock

First Edition

16 17 18 19 20 21 — 9 8 7 6 5 4 3 2 1

Printed in the United States of America

To my wonderful children,
Brennan and Tessa, whose extraordinary
lives bless and enrich mine daily.
In love and service…

"A person begins to live when he learns to live outside of himself. The only man or woman with any chance of happiness is the man or woman who finds a way to serve."

—Albert Einstein

"The best way to find yourself is to lose yourself in the service of others."

—Mahatma Gandhi

Acknowledgments

The writing of this, my second book, has been a blessing for me. Extraordinary Living would not have come to fruition without the creativity and dedication of David Welday, president of HigherLife Development Services.

I'm grateful for David's continuing dialogue with me and for his commitment to ideas and beliefs that truly matter. David's contributions throughout the writing of this book, and the founding of The Service-Driven Institute (www.servicedriveninstitute.com), cannot be overstated.

I am ever grateful for the love and support of my family in my writing and speaking. Bonnie and my children are a constant source of joy in my life. I am very proud of each of them and love each of them dearly.

I remain grateful for and blessed by the power of service—the key to extraordinary living! If you find this book helpful and meaningful, I hope you'll be in touch with me. You'll find contact information in the back of the book. If you believe service is a key, both to extraordinary living and to creating a world filled with love and compassion, consider becoming a member of The Service-Driven Institute ("SDI"). Through the SDI webpage and blog, you can interact with others who have read this book and have been moved and inspired. The mission statement of the SDI is at the back of this book in Appendix 3. For more information, visit www.service-driveninstitute.com.

My great thanks to Libbye Morris, whose editing skills and input have improved this book immeasurably.

In love and in service,
Donald Clinebell
San Clemente, California, USA

Table of Contents

Preface

Not long ago, I found myself standing in the self-improvement section of one of today's few popular "brick and mortar" bookstores. I was drawn by the smell of the books and aromatic coffee that mingled with the attractive book covers. I was struck by the sheer number of books, workbooks, audiotapes, CDs, and DVDs in this section of the bookstore, each designed to "improve" me. What I didn't find was help.

This book is not about self-improvement. But it can help you find what we all want: an abundant life, a life worth living, an empowered life filled with meaning, purpose, and great joy. If you are looking for glib answers to unanswerable questions, this is not the book for you. If you want to get in shape, keep a journal, listen to the right tapes, walk on hot coals, have the right Blackberry, or blueberry, the right iPhone or Droid or anything else, close this book now. But if you are looking for help as you address life's most important questions—or as Walt Whitman so eloquently put it, "What good amid these, O me! O life!"—then read on!

My first book, The Service-Driven Life, was published in 2012. It is about the power of service in the Judeo-Christian belief system and about discovering deep meaning and great joy in that context. The Service-Driven Life contains Christian terminology and teaching. It is, in many ways, a book about my own journey to a service-driven life. What I have come to know in the years since the publication of The Service-Driven Life is that the power of service is by no means limited to a Judeo-Christian platform.

This second book, Extraordinary Living, is a loving study of the power of service in all of our lives, across all boundaries of faith, all major religions, all belief systems, and spiritual disciplines of significance. It is not based on any particular faith or belief system; rather, it presents the power of service and the key to extraordinary living using values-based spirituality. You may well ask, "Just what does that mean?"

Values are the things we believe are important in the way we live our lives. Spirituality is a sense of connection to something bigger than ourselves, typically involving a search for meaning. As such, it is a universal human experience, something that touches us all. It is a human experience that touches us across all boundaries of all belief systems and philosophies—whether those belief systems and philosophies are found in religious faith, New Age philosophy, Eastern mysticism, spiritual wholeness, spiritual source, a creator, a power greater than ourselves, a higher power, or agnostic or atheist thinking.

Values-based spirituality is a sense that our lives have meaning and fulfill some higher purpose bigger than ourselves. It is aligning what is important to you in the way you live your life with something bigger than yourself, thereby discovering deep meaning and great joy. This book is about that very meaning, purpose, joy, fulfillment, and worthiness. It is about the key to extraordinary living and the journey that takes all of us there.

C. S. Lewis once said, "We think our childish toys bring us all the happiness there is, and our nursery is the whole wide world. But something must drive us out of the nursery and into the world of others."

This book is about getting out of the nursery and moving into the world of others—not as conqueror or boss and certainly not as victim or rug to be trampled. It is about emptying ourselves of egoism. It is about leaving that lifestyle of self-absorption and self-focus—and filling our lives in service to others. You may be reading this book at a time of personal loss, pain, sorrow, addiction, or loneliness. Or you may be grasping for joy, peace, a special relationship, or prosperity. We all want an extraordinary life, but finding it may take us to a surprising place! Are we truly willing to seek and find how to serve? Are we willing to serve others in every part of our lives—at home and with family, in vocation, and with our neighbor(s)? Are we truly willing to live as servants? If so, we will find our lives truly empowered, filled with meaning and joy beyond measure. I invite you to discover the keys to an extraordinary life—a life that matters, that makes a difference. I invite you to embrace the power of service. I invite you to embrace the service-driven life!

Chapter 1

An Introduction to the Power of Service in Your Life

"People are not really afraid of dying; they're afraid
of not ever having lived, nor ever having deeply considered
their life's higher purpose, and not ever having stepped into that
purpose and at least tried to make a difference in this world."

—Joseph Jaworski

S
ervice is not an "add-on" to life. It is the core and foundation of worthiness, fulfillment, meaning, purpose, and great joy. Let's explore this.

Picture your life as a circle. Draw a circle, and put in the center of the circle the words "My Life." Now add a wedge to the pie, within the circle of "My Life." Something like this:

The "Me Circle"

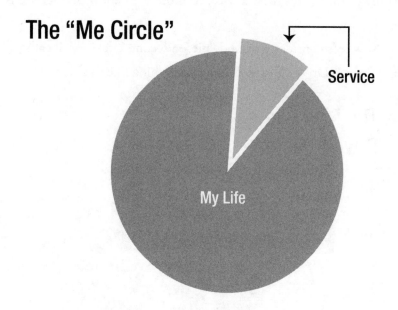

Service

My Life

What you've created in this exercise is an "add-on"—a "service" add-on to the rest of your life. Perhaps the add-on is a substantial block of time, perhaps not. Maybe the service "wedge of the pie" is 7:30 to 8:30 a.m. on a Tuesday morning at a Rotary Club, Kiwanis Club, Optimist Club, or Junior Woman's Club meeting. Or perhaps your service "wedge of the pie" takes place on Sunday morning at the church of your choice. That's good. But consider this: If you live your life in what I call the "Me Circle," you will not and cannot experience the true power of service—the power to change others' lives and your own life. If you live your life in the "Me Circle," you will not live a life that truly matters and truly makes a difference. And you will have missed, in the end, the meaning and joy that come to those driven by service, to those who know that service is at the core.

Now let's consider a second "pie," a second circle. We'll call this the Service-Driven Circle. It looks something like this:

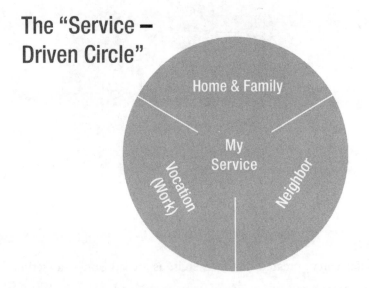

The "Service – Driven Circle"

Notice that within this circle, the word "service" now touches every part of your life—home and family, vocation/work, and neighbor/others. This circle reflects an acknowledgment, a conscious and intentional decision, that everything you do is, or can be, a vessel for service. Yes, everything! As we'll see in the pages of this book, if you choose to live in and with the second circle, the Service-Driven Circle, you will discover a fundamental truth—that service is not an add-on in life. Rather, it is at the core and foundation of worthiness, fulfillment, meaning, purpose, and great joy. It is where the power and indeed the empowerment reside. It's what we are made for. It is the key to extraordinary living!

The Journey Begins

English use of the word "service" creates confusion because of its multiple meanings. Here are some examples: service at a restaurant, service of legal process, a public worship service or religious meeting, a branch of the military, serving balls in tennis, providing maintenance and repair after a sale of goods, providing services as opposed to goods, and providing professional services.

Thankfully, Webster also gives us this definition: "Service: occupation of a servant, of one who serves. Work done or performed for another...an act giving assistance...acting outside of ourselves, outside of ego."[1]

Welcome to the journey, and it is that—a journey—of excitement, purpose, meaning, and joy. In the pages of this book, we will learn how to live an extraordinary life, how to live with purpose and meaning, and how to step into a higher purpose with empowerment and joy. We explore love and service in every part of our lives: With family and friends, those most precious in our lives; in

---

1 *Webster's New World Dictionary*, Third Ed. (1994), 1226.

love and service through vocation, the ways in which we spend the substance of our days; and in love and service for neighbor, literal and figurative. We explore living outside of ourselves and moving into the world of others—men and women of service. Service-driven people.

Someone once asked Albert Einstein, a man with multiple layers of genius, this question: "Who among us makes the greatest contribution to humanity?" His answer: "He who brings out of love a cup of water to a thirsty man."

The amazing miracle—the power, the journey—in this is not the obvious benefit to the thirsty. Rather, it is found in what comes to the one who brings the cup...the true beneficiary. The giver is the one who finds meaning, purpose, energy, and passion for this life, borne of a belief in who we are and what we're doing. The service-driven life yields for the giver—not the one given to—meaning and purpose outside of oneself, as well as passion, hope, and joy within. Those who bring the cup of water begin to line up their values and their spirituality—the beginning of a sense, a peace, that their lives have meaning and fulfill some higher purpose, something bigger than themselves.

There is no human experience more universal than the journey you are about to take. The power of service in your life awaits!

Questions to Think About

■ Right now, is service an "add-on" in your life? If you are ready to live a service-driven life, what will be your first step to make that happen?

_____

_____

_____

■ When you envision a service-driven life that will bring you personal joy, how do you envision being of service in your home and to your family?

_____

_____

_____

■ In your work and vocation?

_____

_____

_____

■ With your neighbor (literal and beyond) and others?

_____

_____

_____

Chapter 2

Out of the Nursery,
Outside of Ourselves

"A person begins to live when he learns to live outside himself."

—Albert Einstein

I t has been said that the difference between ordinary and extraordinary is that little word "extra." Just what is that extra thing, that fundamental shift in the paradigm that changes everything and makes lives not ordinary but extraordinary?

To find the answer, let's look at the story of the Pinto and the Jaguar:

> A Jaguar pulled up to a red stoplight. As the Jaguar driver waited, a lowly Ford Pinto pulled up beside him in the next lane. It was hot, so the windows were down.
>
> "Hey," the Pinto driver said to the Jaguar driver, "nice car. Does it come with a phone? I've got a car phone in my Pinto."
>
> "Well, of course I have a phone in my car—right in the steering wheel, actually," the Jaguar driver said with disdain. "It's built in. Comes from the factory that way."
>
> "Ah," the Pinto driver said. He paused a moment (long stoplight), then said, "I've got a bed in the back of my Pinto. Built in."
>
> "Uh-huh," the Jaguar driver said as the light changed and the Pinto and the Jaguar went their separate ways.
>
> The Jaguar driver was troubled. He couldn't get that Pinto out of his mind. "I spent a fortune on this car," he thought. "I don't have a bed built in. That little Pinto has a bed built in."

So off went the Jaguar driver to the Jaguar dealer. "Hey, look, I spent a fortune here. I want a bed built in—now."

Hector built a bed into the Jaguar.

The Jaguar driver drove off. Over the next few days, he kept a sharp eye out for that Pinto. Days later, in the back of a deserted Kmart parking lot, he spotted the Pinto. He approached. There the Pinto sat, lowly and dirty, windows rolled up. The Jaguar driver got out of his Jaguar and walked up to the Pinto. He noticed that the windows of the Pinto were fogged up.

He knocked on the window…perhaps inadvisably, he knocked again. Nothing. He knocked one last time. Slowly…slowly the back window came down. There was the Pinto driver.

"Hey," the Jaguar driver said, "I got a bed built in my Jaguar!"

The Pinto driver looked at him, irritated, and said simply, "You got me out of the shower to tell me that?"

That's a story about two men in the nursery; it's funny but sad. Extraordinary living is about getting out of the nursery and moving into the world of others. It is about emptying ourselves of egoism, leaving that lifestyle of self-absorption and self-focus, and filling our lives with service to others.

The self-help gurus were wrong. It's not about self-analysis, not about going inside and analyzing and ruminating about ourselves. Rather, it is about learning to step outside of ourselves in service to others, thereby finding deep meaning and great joy, empowered in "the common thread of service" and beginning to live extraordinary lives.

Questions to Think About

■ Looking deep inside yourself, to what extent are you ego-driven? How much of your time and energy do you spend thinking about your own situation and challenges?

_____

_____

_____

■ What is something specific—even if it seems small—that you can do today to step outside of yourself and begin focusing on others? At home? At work? With neighbors?

_____

_____

_____

■ What do you notice in yourself—what do you feel— when you step outside of yourself and serve others? A sense of empowerment, meaning, joy?

_____

_____

_____

Chapter 3

The Common Thread
of Service

"Everybody can be great because anybody can serve.
You don't have to have a college degree to serve.
You don't have to make your subject and verb agree to serve.
You only need a heart full of grace. A soul generated by love."

—Martin Luther King, Jr.

S ervice as a way of living is a framework for our lives. It is a part of every major religion on the planet, yet it transcends every form of religion. It is the common thread of meaning in our lives on this planet. You can find it in true service organizations, twelve-step recovery programs, and most spiritual disciplines and philosophies. Whether you are Christian, Jewish, Buddhist, Muslim, Hindu, New Age, agnostic, or atheist, the power of service is a common thread that is a foundational component of every belief system. We see in this chapter the power of service as the common thread that unites us all.

The Power of Service in the Major Religions and Beyond

Christianity

Service is the foundation of the Christian faith. Christians are commanded to serve, enjoined to love God and to love others as God loves His disciples. (See Ex 20:1–17 and Mark 12:30–31, NRSV.) Jesus of Nazareth said that the two greatest commandments are to love God with all your heart, soul, mind, and strength and to love one another...love your neighbor. We are "sent to serve" (1 Peter 4:10). "As the Father sent me, I send you" (Matt. 25:31–46). "Go where He would go and do what He would do. As you have seen in me, do the same" (Luke 10:1–11). "Little children [all of us], let us love, not in word or speech, but in truth and action" (1 John 3:18).

21

St. Francis of Assisi said, "Preach the gospel at all times, and when necessary, use words."[1]

Those of the Christian faith are sent to make humankind their business. Charles Dickens said, "The common welfare is our business; mercy, charity, and forbearance are our business." Mark 10:43 (NSRV) says, "Whoever wishes to become great must become a servant." And Luke 17:5–10 says, "If you would be great...serve." In Christian terms, we empty ourselves, as Jesus did.

If you want to have a further look at the central role of service on the Christian platform, you may wish to read The Service-Driven Life, a book about the power of service including Christian terminology and teaching. Its central theme is this: God stands at the door and knocks. When a Christian opens the door and lets God in, God "sups" with him or her. The Christian learns that it is in love, compassion, and forgiveness for ourselves and others that one truly serves God. We are led to serve Him by serving others—with constancy, energy, passion, purpose, and joy beyond measure. The biblical base for the book is John 15.

Not only are Christians led to serve by serving others, in every part of their lives; they are commanded to serve by serving others. The word "commandment" does not need to be "off-putting" (in the old English usage). Rather, the word "commandment," a word that once may have suggested rigid rules and orders, now brings to

---

1 . St. Francis of Assisi (1181–1226) is one of the most venerated religious figures in history. He was an Italian Catholic friar and preacher who founded the men's Franciscan Order. Pope Francis took his name from St. Francis. This timeless quotation is in the public domain; it is more than eight hundred years old.

the Christian a life-changing invitation to purpose, meaning, and empowerment. The commandment becomes an invitation to a place of complete joy. In the upper room, as Jesus prepared to "go to Him who sent me" (John 16:5), Jesus told his disciples this: "This is my commandment, that you love one another just as I have loved you" (John 15:12). He also said, "If you keep my commandments, you will abide in my love. I have said these things to you so that my joy may be in you and that your joy may be complete" (John 15:10–11).

For the Christian, service is a way of living commanded by Jesus, but not as a means to heaven and not as "works" justifying us. No! Rather, it is a way to discover that God's joy can be in us, and our joy can be complete.[1] In my faith, salvation, love, and forgiveness come by God's grace. His grace is either free, or it is not. And it most assuredly is—through His "amazing grace." In the Catholic faith, the view of "works" is somewhat different; that theological view is not discussed here. I prefer, rather, the view of Mother Teresa— soon to be a saint within the Catholic church—who said, "I live as a servant, and thereby I am changed; I am renewed."[2]

In the Christian faith, service is not and should not be based in fear and guilt. If the Christian experiences fear and guilt, the

---

1 . For a full discussion of grace and "what service is not," I invite you to read pages 29–31 of *The Service-Driven Life*, available at www.theservice-drivenlife.com. In Christian terms, neither *The Service-Driven Life* nor the Service-Driven Institute suggests in any way that service is a means or a condition of receiving God's grace.

2 . This quote is attributed to Mother Teresa in an interview following her address to the UN General Assembly on October 26, 1984.

anecdote is God's unconditional love—His grace! And in Christian terms, that is good news indeed.

What is also good news is the invitation to serve at home, at work, and with our neighbor. It is an invitation to step outside ourselves, thereby finding deep meaning, purpose, and joy and becoming empowered in service to others.

A further note, and caution on service in the Christian faith. If you come from a Christian tradition and find yourself in a place of doubt and disappointment, lacking faith, know this: You are not alone in that. Many Christian churches out there offer easy solutions to the most difficult questions: What does it mean? What is my purpose? Why am I on this planet? They offer "solutions" that introduce fear, guilt, doubt, and ultimately dangerous and hurtful disappointment.

As a Methodist "preacher's kid," I grew up seeing much of the soft underbelly of the organized church. Not just the petty, oh-so-human bickering, but the need to win souls to make or increase a budget and the need to cement membership. In today's world, the need to twist and manipulate scripture—or designate one's reading of scripture as the only reading—for personal gain is rampant. If you give money, He will richly reward you, or so it goes, financially and with meaning in your life. And, conveniently enough, here's the address to send your "love gift," your investment in your very own future. Boy, are you going to feel a whole lot better having unloaded your life savings to this ministry. This "answer" to life's most important question is at best short-term and, at worst, fraudulent. It is the most blatant form of "religion that hurts."[1]

Sometimes, the answer to "Where is the meaning, where is my purpose?" is phrased in the Christian church as an urgent and fear-based imperative. "Do it our way," is the message in some churches, "or you are hell-bound." That's enough to scare some folks. It is not enough to give us true purpose and meaning.

Love and fear, you see, are inconsistent. Fear is never enough to give us peace. Although it may get us out of bed each day for some period of time, it is in no way a satisfactory answer or a lasting solution to any questions, including those essential to a meaning-filled life. Fear most certainly fails to provide us with any joy in life.

My personal belief system? I do not believe that God, a loving God, offers us fear. God offers us love and forgiveness without condition. That is why we are enjoined, not to fear Him, but to trust Him wholly, fear nothing, hope ever, and look ever up to Him.

---

1 . Howard Clinebell, *Religion That Hurts* (2002). The phrase "religion that hurts" was written by Howard Clinebell, PhD, an ordained Methodist minister; one of the pioneers in the pastoral psychology and counseling movement; the founding professor of pastoral counseling at the Claremont School of Theology; and founder of The Clinebell Institute in Claremont (http://www.theclinebellinstitute.org/). The phrase "religion that hurts" is taken from an outline for a book Dr. Clinebell intended to write. It was tentatively titled *Religion That Heals, Religion That Hurts*. The book would have been added to his list of more than twenty published books. In 2004, there came to Howard Clinebell, my father, "not the final sleep, but the final awakening." The phrase "not the final sleep, but the final awakening" is sometimes attributed to Sir Walter Scott (1771–1835), Scottish author and poet. William J. Bennett's book, The *Book of Virtues,* suggests that the origin of the phrase is actually found in the John Donne poem "Death, Be Not Proud." John Donne (1572–1631) was an English poet, lawyer, and priest.

We are commanded to live good lives, to love God and others, and to serve others. And what does God offer us, indeed promise us? Only to love us, to care for us, and to be with us...forever (Gen. 9:8–17, NRSV). In this text, the word "covenant," or promise, is mentioned seven times in most translations. And He offers to show us His face through the manyfold acts of service we are commanded to embrace.

In the Christian faith, which comes first? God or service? Service or God? A popular Christian book, The Purpose Driven Life by Rick Warren, suggests that the meaning of life rests in living a "purpose driven" life. (Warren has acquired a registered trademark for the phrase "purpose driven.") The book rests on two premises. The first is that "It all starts with God," a Christian God—no question, no argument, no further thought needed. The second premise: God has five "purposes" for our lives. The one way to find meaning is to become a "world-class Christian," through service ("ministry") to the "believers" and service ("mission") to the "unbelievers." The fundamental mission, of course, is said to be to "go and make disciples" of the "unbelievers."

At the risk of incurring the wrath (and the unsolicited prayer) of the "world-class Christians," this single-minded and admittedly very simple approach to "meaning" in life is distinguished only by its narrowness, intolerance, and striking internal inconsistency. It does preach the need to become a servant, to empty oneself of ego, and to overcome self-centeredness. But it is also designed to deal with a world that is 31 percent Christian by making the other 69 percent into Christians. Purpose and meaning are reserved for the Christian world—none for you if you are not a Christian or open to becoming one. (There are nineteen major religions on the face on the planet, and they are subdivided into 270 large religious groups, according to the 2006 US Census.)

This dangerous view yields this disturbing conclusion: "World-class Christians are the only fully alive people on the planet."[1] This leaves a group of "world-class Christians" not only full of ego and judgment, but full up with arrogance and self-centeredness. And it leaves 4.4 billion men, women and children out of this exclusive, "world-class" club. It divides the world into "believers" and "unbelievers" and even divides up "believers." We can almost read between the lines: "There is only one way to be a good Christian and, guess what, it's our way."

Does it all start with God? For some, yes. For others, not even close. For some, it begins with service...humble servants led to the God of their understanding—men and women in service through whom the God of their understanding works. We see this in the stories of service that follow in a later chapter of this book.

The good news is that to find purpose and meaning, we don't have to judge 4.4 billion people. The Christian faith needs to "lose" the judgment, the lack of compassion, the "exclusive club" attitude, and the "superior Christian" mentality; those are not of God. What God commands Christians to embrace is quite the opposite. Judge not. Love others just as I have loved you... and live as a servant that thereby you may be changed, you may be renewed. And that thereby you may see the face of God.

---

1 . Rick Warren, *The Purpose Driven Life*, 298.

We begin to see the thread—service—that runs through the heart of every major religion and belief system on the face of the planet. In terms of adherents, Christianity is the largest religion in the world (approximately 31.5 percent of the world's population, 2.2 billion adherents).[1] We have seen the central role of service in Christianity. Let's have a look at four other major religions.

Judaism

The imperative to serve is woven throughout the Bible's Old Testament. In addition to Exodus 20:1–17, we find this command in Deuteronomy 15:11: "I therefore command you, 'Open your hand to the poor and needy neighbor in your land.'" And Micah 6:8 says, "And what does the Lord require of you but to do justice, and to love kindness, and to walk humbly with your God." Deuteronomy 11–13 and 1 Samuel 12:20 tell us to love God and serve with all one's heart and soul. In the words of the Talmud, the central text of Rabbinic Judaism, "the highest form of wisdom is kindness."

The essential core of Judaism is this: "The holiest preparation we can do for our souls is to do good for others, and in so doing, do good." Helping others helps us.[2]

---

1 . "The Global Religious Landscape," December 18, 2012, Pew Research Center website, http://www.pewforum.org/2012/12/18/global-religious-landscape-exec/?utm_content=bufferf682f&utm_source=buffer&utm_medium=twitter&utm_campaign=Buffer.

2 . Jewish Federation of Metrowest New Jersey, http://www.jfedgmw.org/search?keywords=service+to+others#sthash.C7LvljBX.dpuf.

Islam

Islam is the second largest religion in the world (22 percent of the world's population). The religion is guided by the sayings of the prophet Muhammad, Haditha. This is the religion of 1.6 billion adherents, not the hijacked religion of a relatively small group of evildoers and those who engage in unspeakable terror. In true Islam, we find that the Prophet teaches service: "No man is a true believer unless he desires for his brother that which he desires for himself." Essentially the Golden Rule, love thy neighbor as you would be loved. "The creation is like God's family...the most beloved unto God is the person who does good to God's family."[1]

Hinduism

The Hindu religion is the third largest on the planet, with 14 percent of the world's population, approximately one billion people, as adherents. Perhaps the oldest of the world's religions, at its heart is the "creator spirit," embodying service to and respect for others as a key part of Hindu life. In the words of Mahatma Gandhi, "The best way to find yourself is to lose yourself in the service of others."

As in Islam, the Golden Rule is also key to Hinduism as the sum of all true righteousness. This truth is written in the Mahabharata,

---

1 . *The Truth About Islam* (Washington, DC: The Wisdom Fund, 2003), www.twf.org.

an ancient Indian epic poem.[1] The founder of the Self-Realization Fellowship, a Hindu-based "fellowship," said, "You should serve others as you serve God."[2]

Buddhism

Buddhism is the world's fourth-largest religion, with 5.2 percent of the population (approximately 376 million people) adhering to its beliefs. Buddhism teaches a "triple truth," attributed to Hindu Prince Gautama Siddhartha (564–483 BC), the founder of Buddhism. He said, "Teach this truth to all: A generous heart, kind speech, and a life of service are the things that renew humanity." The Udānavarga is an early Buddhist collection of topically organized chapters (Sanskrit: varga) of aphoristic verses or "utterances" (Sanskrit: udāna) attributed to Buddha and his disciples. Section 5.18 addresses what amounts to a Buddhist version of the Golden Rule: "Treat not others in ways that you would find hurtful."[3]

---

1 . "Mahabharata" is one of two works considered sacred scripture in Hinduism; the other is "Ramayana," a Sanskrit epic poem ascribed to the Hindu sage and Sanskrit poet Valmiki.

2 . Paramahansa Yogananda, *Sayings of Paramahansa Yogananda,* Los Angeles: Self-Realization Fellowship Publishing, (1980), 34.

3 . Franz Bernhard, Udānavarga, Section 5.18, Band I, Sanskrittexte aus den Turfanfunden X, Vandenhoeck & Ruprecht, Göttingen (1965).

The Common Thread that Unites Us

The common thread—service to others—runs through the major religions. It runs through all belief systems of consequence. Let's look at some of those.

New Age Philosophy

New Age philosophy covers a broad spectrum of thinking, generally thought to have originated in the 1970s. It includes an eclectic range of spiritual beliefs. It also includes the common thread of service. The well-known author and PBS presenter, Wayne Dyer, is a good example of New Age thinking, which has at its core service to others. During his lifetime, and during his career, Dyer spoke frequently about "source," "divine connection," "spiritual center," a "universal spirit." Although Dyer sometimes quoted from scripture, and sometimes used the word "God," his conception of a source, a God, was not aligned with any major religion. His philosophy was in essence Eastern-influenced metaphysical thought. In this sense, he was "New Age."

Although some may argue that Dyer's approach to source, spirit, God was inconsistent and difficult to discern, the Eastern influence on Dyer is undeniable. He said, "Service to others is one of the four cardinal virtues described by Lao-tzu…extend yourself in a spirit of giving, helping, or loving…."[1]

---

1 . "The Healing Power of Service," June 2010, Wayne Dyer blog, http://www.drwaynedyer.com/blog. Enter "the healing power of service" in the search box on the blog page.

In 2013, two years before his death, Dyer wrote this: "How may I serve? Asking this question can turn your life around. Thinking of others first—reaching out to them despite how it might inconvenience you—causes you to feel joy. This gift of feeling good (or feeling God) within comes from serving and surrendering rather than asking and demanding."[1]

This almost agnostic approach—the assumption that we cannot know the true nature of God; we can only know our approach to our source, our Creator—was the very nature of Dyer's thinking and writing. His endpoint? If we align ourselves with our source, whether within or without of ourselves, we will find happiness. And extending ourselves in service to others is the very nature of our source, our Creator. Our service is what Dyer referred to as a part of our "power of intention," creating our world consistent with four cardinal virtues.

Dyer, who died in 2015, was not without his critics. Some contended that Dyer's view was more that the world served him. That Dyer's conceptual model was that by aligning himself with source, with creator, the world then served him. The world brought into a state of peace and happiness through pure "intention" and within self.

Other critics have objected that by broadcasting Dyer's hours-long specials on his books, the Public Broadcasting System was at least impliedly endorsing his view of the world. PBS, interestingly, responded to these critics by painting a picture of Dyer as simply a nice man with some great stories to tell. People liked him, they felt

---

1 . Wayne Dyer, November 29, 2013, Facebook post, https://www.facebook.com/drwaynedyer/posts/10152026361881030.

better after hearing him, and they felt connected to something bigger than themselves. Spiritually, what could be more New Age than that?

Servant-Based Leadership/Spirituality

Robert Greenleaf (1904–90) is considered the founder of the "servant-based leadership" movement. However, his thinking went way beyond the field of leadership. Certainly Greenleaf constructed an amazing dynamic for leadership.

Yes, true leaders are "servants." But it is more. Joseph Jaworski, author of Synchronicity, says, "The essence of leadership is the desire to serve one another and to serve something beyond ourselves, a higher purpose." It sounds a lot like spirituality, with service at its core—that is, seeking something bigger than ourselves. Again, it's a universal journey and search.

Greenleaf tells the story of Leo, taken from Herman Hesse's book Journey to the East. As recounted by Jaworski:

> The narrator of the story is on a journey with a band of men, looking for enlightenment… Leo is the servant who does the group's mental chores but who also sustains them with his presence, his spirit, and his song. The journey lasts for years, and all goes well until Leo disappears. The group finds they cannot make it without Leo. They fall into disarray, they become lost, and the narrator almost dies. After years of wandering, the narrator finally finds Leo and is taken to the order that sponsored the journey. There, Greenleaf says, he discovers that Leo, whom he had first known as servant,

was actually the head of the order, its guiding spirit, a great and noble leader. Leo, by the quality of the inner life that was expressed in his presence, had served to lift the group up and make their journey possible.[1]

"Guiding spirit," "serving something bigger than ourselves," a spiritual journey." In Greenleaf's work, in the early to mid-twentieth century, we find a kind of spirituality, a kind of New Age thinking before its time, with service at its core and as a common thread of meaning.

Science-Based Thinking

As unlikely as it may seem—and this is where the power of service and its capacity to cross all lines and boundaries of belief and nonbelief becomes truly amazing—we find the common thread of service in the thinking of the most brilliant and accomplished scientists in human history, all outside of any faith base. Three examples are Einstein, Edison, and Schweitzer.

Einstein is the most prominent example. He said, "A person begins to live when he learns to live outside of himself. The only man with any chance of happiness is the man who finds a way to serve." Albert Schweitzer said, "The only ones among you who will be truly happy are those who will have sought and found how to serve." Two of the most brilliant scientific and medical minds of the past four centuries were focused on service as the way to meaning and "happiness."

---

1 . Joseph Jaworski, *Synchronicity: The Inner Path of Leadership* (San Francisco: Berrett-Koehler Publishers, 2011), 58–59.

Thomas Edison, a true man of science, secured 1,309 patents in his lifetime. And these were patents on important developments: the telephone, the telegraph, the phonograph, the lightbulb, and harnessing electricity. These were monumental inventions that changed the world forever and, most would say, for the better.

And what was Edison's view of what he accomplished? When asked how he managed to secure so many patents on so many inventions, he responded that most people miss the opportunities because the opportunities "come dressed in overalls and look like work." When asked why he worked so hard at his inventions? "It's fun" was his first response. Then…this: "I have never perfected an invention that I did not think about in terms of the service it might give others…I find out what the world needs, then I proceed to invent."

So even brilliant minds and scientific thinking are connected by the common thread of service, a common value by which brilliant and scientific minds have discovered meaning and purpose in life.

Einstein was a supremely rational and scientific mind, and he was an avowed agnostic in his early years. Yet in seeking the truth about the cosmos and its construct, he found his way, or was led, to a power greater than himself, to a God of his understanding. As a man of service, Einstein reached a fascinating conclusion and "religious" endpoint. For more on this topic, see Chapter 10.

Agnostic Thinking

Agnosticism is not a religion. In its most fundamental form, it is a way of thinking, a skepticism about what we as humans can know or do know. It is a concept, an approach, a belief related to the existence or nonexistence of God. However...

Agnosticism through the centuries has incorporated a moral code, a belief system that incorporates features similar to the attributes of religion. Consider these sources: In the first century, Marcus Aurelius, a Stoic philosopher and Roman emperor, wrote, "If there are gods and they are just, then they will not care how devout you have been but will welcome you based on the virtues you have lived by. If there are no gods, then you will be gone but will have lived a noble life that will live on in the memories of your loved ones."

In 1860, Abraham Lincoln said, "When I do good, I feel good; when I do bad, I feel bad. That's my religion."

In 2011, Joseph Bugliosi, an attorney and the author of Divinity of Doubt: The God Question, wrote, "There is only one necessary religion that has any merit to the people who inhabit this earth, and that's the Golden Rule: 'Whosoever ye would that men should do to you, do ye even so to them.' To treat others as you would want them to treat you (the only obvious exception being when acting in any kind of self-defense) is the highest, most noble form of human behavior and the basis of all morality."

Thus, we see that even in agnostic thinking, service is a common thread, a common value by which the agnostic finds meaning and purpose. "Do unto others." Serve. It's what we're made for.

Atheist Thinking

Atheism is also not a religion. In its most fundamental form, it is a way of thinking; a denial of the existence of God and of any faith base or theological basis for moral behavior. It is not a belief system. However...

Atheist thinking has developed a basic tenet that does indeed incorporate morality. In particular, it is a moral dimension not based on any theological belief, but rather a moral dimension "boiled down to one simple piece of guidance, which is commonly referred to as the "golden rule."[1] Many atheists behave in "moral" or "compassionate" ways because they feel a natural tendency to empathize with other humans. In such thinking, the derivation of that code of conduct has nothing to do with religion, God, or faith; rather for the atheist, this is a code of conduct, a "morality" that "we as a species could have figured out...on our own."[2]

Thus we see that even in atheist thinking, service is a common thread, a common value by which the atheist finds meaning and purpose. "Do unto others." Serve. It's what we're made for.

Service Organizations

The common thread of service runs, of course, through every true service organization. This may seem self-evident. But the

---

1 . Amy L. Hansmann, Brainerd, Minnesota, Dispatch op-ed, March 12, 2015.

2 . Ibid.

power of service is nowhere more evident than in the story of Rotary International. The organization has 33,000 clubs worldwide, where men and women are driven by a powerful approach to living: "Service above self."

Rotary and clubs like it are referred to as "service" clubs. Just what does that mean, for those who serve and those who are served? More than one hundred years ago, four men in Chicago, Illinois—a lawyer, a coal distributor, a merchant tailor, and a mining engineer—met for the very first time to found a club that would go on to become Rotary, "rotating" its meeting place between and among member business locations. This was more than a club; it was a service club. It was an organization of four businessmen in Chicago that would go on to become the largest and most accomplished service organization on the face of the planet. It is now composed of 1.2 million professional businessmen and women in nearly two hundred countries united not by a religion, but by a commitment to service—"service above self." They are not Christian Rotarians, Jewish Rotarians, or Muslim Rotarians; they are simply Rotarians…in service.

In the end, we begin to see service as the thread that runs through every major religion, every recovery movement, every spiritual philosophy and discipline, every belief system of consequence. That common thread is what reveals to us the very power of service and what that power can do in our lives. In short, it can transform us from lives that are unfulfilled, lacking in purpose and meaning, and lacking even a modicum of joy, to extraordinary lives—lives that matter, make a difference, and are filled with joy without measure. Whether your belief system is found in the major religions or in New

Age philosophy, in Eastern mysticism, in spiritual wholeness, in a spiritual source, in scientific thinking, in servant-based leadership/ spirituality, or in agnostic or atheist thinking, the power of service is for you!

Questions to Think About

■ Have you ever had a less-than-positive experience with organized religion? If so, can you see yourself living a life of service outside the constructs of a church or other organized religious group? How?

_____

_____

_____

■ Of the service organizations listed in Appendix 1, which of them resonate with you? Consider beginning your service-driven life by volunteering for an organization that needs you.

_____

_____

_____

■ How would you define your belief system? Is it based in one of the major religions, or in New Age philosophy, in Eastern mysticism, in spiritual wholeness, in a spiritual source, in scientific thinking, in servant-based leadership/spirituality, or in agnostic or atheist thinking? Does your belief system include the "common thread" of service?

_____

_____

_____

■ How would it feel to align what you believe is important in the way you live your life—your values—with
a higher purpose, something bigger than yourself?

_____

_____

_____

Chapter 4:

Stories of Service: Empowered to Live with Meaning and Joy

"I live as a servant, and thereby I am changed; I am renewed."

—Mother Teresa

So what do you do when day breaks tomorrow morning and you'd rather not put your feet on the floor to face another day? If life seems to be losing its day-to-day joy for you, read on.

Consider the power—the meaning, the joy—found in the following stories of service. As you read, allow yourself to feel the power of the stories—the meaning and the joy not only in those who are served, but in those who serve. Notice the common thread found in those who serve and in those who focus not on the receiving but on the giving.

Restoring Sight to the Blind

A twenty-nine-year-old woman in India was the mother of a six-year-old boy and a four-year-old girl. This young mother was blind and had been since birth. A service club from the United States found the time, money, and energy to send surgical instruments and a surgeon to India to help restore her sight. All services connected with the surgery were donated.

The surgery was delicate, risky, and difficult. After ten hours of surgery and hours upon hours of recovery, the mother slowly opened her eyes and began to weep. Not just because she could see for the first time...but because for the first time ever, she laid eyes upon her son and daughter, ages six and four.

The mother's tears of joy were shared by tears of joy in the surgeon, who later said this, "I believe I know how that surgery changed that young mother and her two children. But what I know without doubt is that I am changed, I am renewed."

45

Tears of joy. The power of service.[1]

Healing the Sick—Eradication of the Wild Polio Virus

In 1987, Rotary International made a commitment to eradicate the wild polio virus from the face of the planet. Over a period of eighteen years, 2.2 billion polio vaccines were administered worldwide, resulting in a 99 percent drop in new cases. Today, as the world stands on the brink of the eradication of polio, an estimated six million children walk the planet polio-free because men and women of service were there, and only because men and women of service were there.

Look in the eyes of any one of those children—walking, playing, and living polio-free. And look in the eyes of those men and women donating their services to administer donated polio vaccines to children all over this world. What you will see is the power of service.

Feeding the Hungry

All over this world, throughout the year, the same scene is repeated, over and over…food and toy drives. A child takes a holiday meal with her family who otherwise would partake only of bread, water, and a few beans. In just one small service club, 140 boxes of food, one each for 140 families averaging four family members each adds

---

1 . This man of service prefers to remain anonymous but has given permission for this story to be told. His work includes many surgeries every year, without charge, in third-world countries around the globe.

up to 140 x 4 lives changed—560 lives! Imagine that a child in your town had never received a Christmas present—till there was you!

Read that last sentence: "Imagine that a child in your town had never received a Christmas present—till there was you!" Feel the meaning, the joy. Feel the power of service!

Changing Lives through Youth Programs

The following poem by poet Will Allen Dromgoole depicts well the power of helping others find their way, even if those nearby question such a gesture:

> An old man, going a lone highway,
> Came at the evening, cold and gray
> To a chasm, vast and deep and wide,
> Through which was flowing a sullen tide.
> The man crossed in the twilight dim—
> That sullen stream had no fears for him;
> But he turned when he reached the other side
> And built a bridge to span the tide.
>
> "Old man," said a fellow pilgrim near,
> "You are wasting strength in building here.
> Your journey will end with the ending day;
> You never again must pass this way.
> You have crossed the chasm, deep and wide,
> Why build you the bridge for the eventide?"

The builder lifted his old gray head.
"Good friend, in the path I have come," he said,
"There followeth after me today
A youth whose feet must pass this way.
This chasm that has been naught to me
To that fair-haired youth may a pitfall be.
He too must cross in the twilight dim;
Good friend, I am building the bridge for him."

—"The Bridgebuilder"
Will Allen Dromgoole, American Poet

Reading programs, after-school programs, youth camps, mentoring and tutoring…thousands upon thousands of such programs exist worldwide. They are changing lives every day. In California, kids at risk for failure in middle schools are tutored and mentored by busy professionals. Mentors serve as success models. A general contractor helps a student get organized for middle school. A lawyer helps a student with science homework. A female orthodontist talks to a young girl about the nexus between school and future success. Successful role models working one on one with students on campus are effective because those types of efforts are making a difference. It's the right thing to do, and the tutors/mentors are getting as much out of the program as the kids are. For some of these kids, these are the first consistently present adults in their lives.

Those in service serve pizza and soda to the kids once a month and just talk to the kids. Mentoring events are held off campus. Kids are presented with awards and recognition. Their grade point averages improve. Kids' parents are so moved by the program that they declare a new intention to value and improve their parenting. Extraordinary mentors everywhere are service-driven, and see their own lives changed forever by the power of service. But before we look at the amazing stories of mentoring and tutoring—and their impact on those who are served and those who serve—here are some grim statistics.

It is no secret that we have in the United States, and in other countries, an epidemic of children without positive role models. This is no longer a matter of dispute. Every US president since Carter, of every political stripe, has talked about this epidemic. We are talking about single-parent families, no-parent families, and homes in which parents are not parenting.

Many of the kids in mentoring/tutoring programs come from such homes; many have no positive male influence in the home. Some live with a grandmother, an aunt, or a single parent. Many, if not most, come from severely dysfunctional families.

It is also no secret that these kids are overwhelmingly at risk for failure, dropping out of school, drugs, crime, and gangs. Kids without positive role models will find role models, but they are unlikely to be positive. Nationwide, and around the world, we are reaping the result of the epidemic—this absence of positive role models. Listen to these statistics:

According to the US Department of Justice, juvenile arrests in 2014 were a staggering 1.1 million kids, ages ten to seventeen.[1] In a poll taken at the California Youth Authority in Chino, California, 35 percent of youth incarcerated there believe it is "OK to shoot a person if that is what it takes to get something you want." Well, that's just kids in jail, you say? Consider this: Ten percent of all Orange County, California, students polled thought it was "OK to shoot a person if that is what it takes to get something you want."[2]

More than 26 percent of violent crime, including homicides, in California is committed by kids eighteen and under. The Young and the Ruthless. In 2014, there were 27,651 felony arrests in California; 1,427 of those were homicide arrests.[3] That's approximately 7,000 arrests just in California for violent felonies in the age group ten to seventeen; there were 400 homicide arrests in the same age group.

What can we do? We can throw up our hands and blame the parents (absent or present). We can whine and moan about it and pour ourselves another drink. We can wallow in cynicism and fear. We can build bigger walls around our homes, leave these kids in the lurch, and see what happens.

Or we can choose to serve. We can choose the power of service. We can choose to make a difference. We can believe that the quality

---

1 . Melissa Sickmund and Charles Puzzanchera, "Juvenile Offenders and Victims: 2014 National Report," National Center for Juvenile Justice and Office of Juvenile Justice and Delinquency Prevention, December 2014, http://www.ojjdp.gov/ojstatbb/nr2014/downloads/NR2014.pdf.

2 . "California Attorney General's Report on Homicide," 2014, https://oag. ca.gov/crime.

3 . Ibid.

of our own lives, and certainly that of our children, will depend on how well we prepare all children for their future.

You see, mentoring and tutoring programs are designed to address the epidemic one child at a time. The following stories demonstrate the power of service in action; both feature young people who were mentored and tutored as a part of a Rotary Club's 7th-Inning Stretch Program.

Kevin's Story

Kevin lived with his mom in a dysfunctional single parent family. There was no positive male presence in the home, and no real parenting was going on. He entered the 7th-Inning Stretch Program, a mentoring and tutoring program for middle-school kids at risk in San Clemente, California, as a "D" and "F" student. He was on the verge of failure. Although English is his primary language, he was virtually unable to speak—or wouldn't speak—at school. Kevin was truly unable to cope with school. He had high absenteeism, low reading skills, frequent disciplinary problems, and yes—even in middle school—a tendency toward gang activity.

In the fall of 1995, Kevin entered the program. He began to receive tutoring...slowly. He participated, quietly at first, in mentoring events. He had lunch with the mentors once a month, just to talk... ever so little at first...and then something began to change: Kevin began to speak to his tutor/mentor to ask a question...to accept help in getting organized....to talk about what he was interested in, about what might be his passion in terms of a career. And about why this whole "school thing" matters. And finally…the best part of all—he smiled.

Within two and a half school quarters, Kevin became an "A" student. Not only was he coping; he was excelling. He went on to become the program's Student of the Year that year. He and his mom were asked to, and did, attend the program's year-end banquet. At the outset, he had been a young man who was unable to speak at school. And on that day, he spoke eloquently to ninety attendees about his experience in the 7th-Inning Stretch Program and its impact on his life.

Kevin's mom attended with him and was so moved that she declared a new intention to improve her parenting. Talk about a defining moment.

Fast-forward five years. Kevin went on to graduate from high school with honors and attended Princeton University on a full academic scholarship. He no longer needs a tutor. I am honored to say…I am still his mentor.

And the impact on the mentor? As I write this, a tear in my eye becomes a tear on my cheek. The meaning, the joy, and the power of service in my life charges and renews me. I begin to live when I learn to live outside of myself.

Josh's Story

Josh lived with his grandmother, who was struggling with alcoholism. With no parent anywhere to be found, Josh was truly programmed for failure…in middle school and in life. Josh turned it around with the help of the 7th-Inning Stretch middle-school mentoring and tutoring program, featuring men and women in service to middle-schoolers. Five years after graduating from the program, Josh wrote down some thoughts about the impact of what he had experienced in 7th-Inning in a letter to his mentor and tutor about the power of service. Read this writing from Josh, all of seventeen years old:

"To my mentor in the 7th-Inning Stretch:

When you thought I wasn't looking, I saw you frame my first attempt at drawing, and I immediately wanted to draw another.

When you thought I wasn't looking, I saw you bring pizza to our middle school, expecting nothing in return, and I learned that those little things can be the special things in life.

When you thought I wasn't looking, I heard you say a prayer, and I knew there is a God I could always talk to. I learned to trust in God.

When you thought I wasn't looking, I saw you send a card to a friend who was sick, and I learned that we all have to help take care of each other.

When you thought I wasn't looking, I saw you give of your time and money to help people who had nothing, and I learned that those who have something should give to those who don't.

When you thought I wasn't looking, I saw you take care of your home and everyone in it, and I learned that we have to take care of what we are given.

When you thought I wasn't looking, I saw how you handled your responsibilities, even when you didn't feel good, and I learned that I would have to be responsible when I grow up.

When you thought I wasn't looking, I saw tears in your eyes, and I learned that sometimes things hurt, but it's alright to cry.

When you thought I wasn't looking, I saw that you cared, and I wanted to be everything I could be.

When you thought I wasn't looking, I learned most of life's lessons that I need to be a good person when I grow up.

When you thought I wasn't looking, I looked at you and wanted to say, 'Thanks, my Rotary friend, for all the things I saw when you thought I wasn't looking.'"

This young man's life was completely turned around by a Rotary man of service. That is indeed the power of service. But there is more: Try to read Josh's piece without tears of joy. Feel the very power of the words, the meaning and joy in a young man who was served, and the joy in a man who tries to live as a servant. Who in the end is changed? Who is renewed?

Aligning What Is Important with a Higher Purpose

I joined Rotary in 1992 because the organization was making a difference. But it was more. It was something very powerful and, yes, something very loving. There was something about the way Rotary makes a difference. Rotary, you see, is a group of men and women in service. Many are men and women of faith. In fact, twenty-five different faiths, including Christianity, Judaism, Buddhism, Hinduism, and Islam, are reflected in the membership of Rotary International. These are men and women who, in a symbolic sense, "sing"—not just any music, but the music of "those who are climbing to the light," to quote Victor Hugo in Les Miserables.

What do surgery in India, two billion polio vaccines, food and toy drives, mentoring, and tutoring all have in common? Yes, lives that are changed forever, some in miraculous ways. These are stories of service in which "meaningful coincidences" abound and the miracles seem to "show up." Yes, the lives of those who are served are changed.

But in a very profound way, the lives of those who serve are also changed forever. Whether you are a person of faith, whether you believe in a spiritual power greater than yourself or not, the words of Mother Teresa ring true: "I live as a servant, and thereby I am changed; I am renewed." It is the common thread in all of the stories of service and how service empowers those who serve to live with meaning, purpose, and great joy.

And in these stories of service, we find service-driven men and women who have aligned the values that are important to them in the way they live their lives with a higher purpose—with something bigger than themselves. And what does this produce? Certainly a peace beyond understanding, a sense that our lives have meaning and fulfill some larger purpose. But it is more. The power of service creates extraordinary lives, rich with fulfillment and worthiness, and steeped in meaning, purpose, and great joy, beyond all imagining.

Questions to Think About

■ What are your core values in life? What service-related activities would align with those values?

_____

_____

_____

■ What types of service would bring you the most significant feelings of accomplishment? Working with at-risk children? Seniors? Those who need medical attention? Prisoners in need of spiritual guidance? What can you commit to becoming involved in?

_____

_____

_____

■ Think about what Mother Teresa meant when she lived as a servant: "I am changed, I am renewed." To what extent do you think a life of service can change and renew you?

_____

_____

_____

Chapter 5

Service in Recovery

Alcoholics Anonymous (AA) has as its foundation the Big Book. Its official title is Alcoholics Anonymous, The Story of How Many Thousands of Men and Women Have Recovered from Alcoholism. How have they recovered, and how are they recovering? Through seeking and trusting a God of their understanding and then by serving others.

In times of deepest pain, the alcoholic is asked to serve others. He or she is asked to step out of him or herself and his or her difficulties. He plants shade trees; he takes a cup of water to a thirsty man. He comes out of self-centeredness, out of ego, and into His will... And when he has reached at least a beginning of recovery, he is enjoined by the twelfth step of recovery—to serve others. Enjoined to serve others...taking love and healing to others. The Big Book says, "Having had a spiritual awakening as a result of these steps, we tried to carry this message to others..."[1]

The power of recovery—and the peace and serenity that accompany recovery—lies in seeking and trusting the God of one's understanding, in a spiritual awakening—and in serving others. There is a powerful lesson in that.

In AA, every day of every year, recovering alcoholics seek and find the God of their understanding, a power greater than themselves. Bill Wilson, a cofounder of AA, wrote this about alcoholism: "Without help, it is too much for us. But there is one who has all

---

1 . Alcoholics Anonymous, *The Story of How Many Thousands of Men and Women Have Recovered from Alcoholism*, fourth ed. (New York: Alcoholics Anonymous World Services, Inc., 2001), 59.

power—that one is [a power greater than ourselves, the God of our understanding]." May you find Him now!"[1]

The AA Big Book eloquently describes it this way: "What is this but a miracle of healing? Yet its elements are simple. Circumstances made him willing to believe. He humbly offered himself to his Creator—then he knew." To this man, the revelation was sudden. Some of us grow into it more slowly. But He has come to all who have honestly sought Him. We drew near to Him; He disclosed Himself to us!"[2]

The story is told of a man who was moved to stop drinking. One day, a heavy weight was lifted from his shoulders, and a still small voice said only this: "It is done. You have another chance…to live." The man left the nursery and took his story in service to others, in a powerful testimony about deep meaning and great joy.

Al-Anon is a recovery program for those people who are affected by the disease of alcoholism in another person. Its purpose is to help families of alcoholics. It is a program about the "courage to change me." It is about choices. It is about choosing to live not in fear, resentment, and anger but rather in love, caring, and service.

Its twelve steps are the same as those of AA. It too is a spiritual program, and its twelfth step is also based on service, on carrying the message to others. Al-Anon is a program designed not only to help people acknowledge powerlessness over someone else's alcohol; it is a program to help people find themselves and find a different

---

1 . Ibid., 59.

2 . Ibid, 57.

way to live based on love and compassion—for oneself and thus for others. It's all about understanding and acknowledging the unconditional love of a power greater than oneself and discovering love and compassion for oneself.

If you find yourself in recovery, know this: The common thread of service is at the core of the twelve-step recovery movement. In the tenth step, it becomes clear that to sustain recovery and a new and wonderful life, self-searching must become a regular habit. The AA founders wrote that such self-searching, such daily personal inventory, must include asking daily a very important question: Am I doing to others as I would have them do to me—today? Once again, the Golden Rule.

And then there is the twelfth step, the only step to include reference to a "spiritual awakening." This final step, the twelfth step, is in major part about service to others—turning outward to fellow alcoholics and "Al-Anons," and "experiencing the kind of giving that asks no reward." Service to others—"devoted service to family, friends, business and community," practiced in "all one's affairs"— thus becomes an essential part of maintaining recovery and growing in a "spiritual experience." Once again, we see the power of service to empower and to bring deep meaning and great joy. If recovery is where you are in your journey, you have an incredible opportunity—to change your way of living, now not only clean and sober but living life with a joy you never even imagined was possible. Extraordinary living; may it be so in your life.

Questions to Think About

■ Have you ever struggled with addiction to alcohol or drugs, or has anyone close to you? If so, to what extent did you become familiar with Alcoholics Anonymous or Al-Anon?

_____

_____

_____

■ If you are in recovery, when the time comes to look at the tenth and twelfth steps of a twelve-step program, think about the role of service in your recovery and in your life. How do you think service can help you heal? See *Twelve Steps and Twelve Traditions*, Alcoholics Anonymous World Services, Inc., New York, New York, 79th printing (2014), pages 88-95 and page 106-125.

_____

_____

_____

Chapter 6

The Most Important
Question in Your Life: Are
You Living as a Servant?

I t all starts with service. If the guiding principle of your life is service and you are grounded in service in every part of your life, you will find meaning, purpose, and, in the words of the late journalist Max Lerner, an "inner strength that survives all hurt." You will find a strength that not only survives all hurt but enables you to grow in relationships and with a power greater than yourself, even in the midst of the deepest pain and difficulty. And you will find joy beyond measure.

Some start with a concept of God and feel compelled to serve. Others simply serve and thereby find a power greater than themselves…a relationship with the God of their understanding. Many of us don't find a power greater than ourselves. He finds us…in the midst of service, in the eyes of a child, in the eyes of a mother healed by the power of surgeons—the power of service.

Service is the word. It is the common thread of meaning in our lives on this planet. It is what we are made for in all realms: in the world's most popular religions, in true service organizations, in twelve-step recovery programs, in science-based thinking, in servant-based spirituality, in agnosticism and atheism—the common thread.

Albert Einstein, a man of science and of service, said, "The only man [or woman] with any chance of happiness is the man [or woman] who finds a way to serve."

Consider Janet's story. Janet participated in a food and toy drive in her rural hometown. She recruited nine volunteers. A child in her town opened a Christmas gift she otherwise would not have received. A child who otherwise would go hungry took a holiday meal with her family. Just ten volunteers rallied together 140 boxes of food and 140 boxes of toys and gave one of each to 140 families averaging 4 family members each—140 x 4 lives changed! That's 560 lives! In a matter of two years, the program became a model for other food and toy drives in other towns, states, countries, and around the globe.

That's my version of Janet's story. Let's rewind now and hear Janet in her own words:

"I believed I was nothing, worthless. My head told me exactly that, and, boy, did I believe it for years—no, for decades. In my 30's, I was divorced, childless, feeling caught in a job I hated. Caught in an existence without meaning. I was severely depressed and sometimes suicidal.

One day, I was invited to participate in a food and toy drive for a local charity. The same invitation had been given me several years running. I had consistently said no. For some reason, this time, I said yes. And I got to work, recruiting volunteers and organizing. We served many families.

I saw tears in the eyes of those we served; I saw humility, gratefulness, joy in a mother and her small children in my own town—my own state and country—who did not know from where the next meal was coming. After the drive was over, I realized that I had seen something else. In those I served, I had seen the face of God—a Higher Power—and suddenly I knew it. It scared me at first, but it also gave me the quiet comfort of a Higher Power moving in my life. In my life! Extraordinary! I was driven to agree to chair the next drive and to grow the project.

Over time, and with a power greater than myself, I began to learn about love and compassion for others—and for myself. As I learned, and as my thinking changed, I found myself alive with love and compassion for others, moved by a purpose and a joy that filled me up every day—a joy I could never have imagined!"

My friends, Janet discovered the power of service, and the service-driven life. This changes everything!

Questions to Think About

■ Have you ever felt called, compelled, or pulled to serve others in some way? Did you heed that call? Why or why not?

_____

_____

_____

■ Do you personally believe that living a service-driven life can lead you to experience significant meaning and joy in your own life? How?

_____

_____

_____

■ What kind of shift in your thinking would it take to be "of service" at home and with your family, and at work?

_____

_____

_____

■ What opportunities exist in your local area to get involved in service to neighbors—a food, toy, or coat drive? Reading to seniors or young children? Holding newborns at the hospital? Visiting elderly people who are homebound?

_____

_____

_____

Chapter 7

The Service-Driven Life: Change Your Thinking, Change Your Priorities

"Day breaks,
And the boy wakes up
And the dog barks,
And the bird sings
And the sap rises
And the angels sigh…"

—James Taylor, "Copperline"

Whaat will you do when day breaks tomorrow morning and you'd rather not put your feet on the floor to face another day? Perhaps the song of the bird and the bark of the dog seem distant, and angels seem to be a myth from childhood fairy tales. If life seems to be losing its day-to-day joy for you, your life is about to improve—you are beginning a wonderful and life-changing journey.

Think of the happiest person you know. The person who seems to live life with energy, passion, and joy. That is, I submit, the person who understands the power of service and knows that the meaning, purpose, and joy in life are found in service.

The story is told of a lifelong missionary who lived in the poverty and squalor of India for more than fifty years. Late in her life, she was asked a simple but profound question: "How can you live with such energy and passion in the midst of this pain and suffering?" Her answer: "I live as a servant to others, and thereby I am changed; I am renewed." Such a person has no time for dark reflection, depression, fear, and self-doubt. Such a person sees meaning and purpose "without" herself, and passion and hope within.

Does this mean that each of us must seek meaning and joy and renewal in mission work in a far-off land? In self-denial, among pain and suffering? No. Some are called to such work; they are indeed the angels among us.

For most of us, our quest for meaning and joy means taking an honest personal inventory and it means a little or a lot of "reordering." Here are three steps for finding out what is most important in life.

1. Reorder Your Thinking

"If you keep on saying things are going to be bad,
you have a good chance of being a prophet."
—Isaac Singer

The first step is to reorder your thinking. What goes on in the six inches between your ears? When you think about your life and the meaning of what you do, are you defeated before you begin?

Do you see what you do every day as meaningless, worthless, hopeless? That kind of thinking locks us in a very dark and lonely room, full of fear, doubt, and self-judgment. As you'll see in later chapters (Chapter 8, "Serving through Love and Compassion," and Chapter 9, "Think Differently, Do Differently"), our thinking can control and smother us, or it can free us. Are you living a life of "quiet desperation?" Or are you living a life filled with passion, energy, and joy? Do you truly believe that what you do is worthy? That everything you do is, or can be, a vessel for service?

"The true measure of a man (or woman) has nothing to do
with status. Life is not about prestige; it is about passion
and purpose. It is about impacting the lives of others."
—Jeffrey Marx, Author of The Long Snapper:
A Second Chance, a Super Bowl, a Lesson for Life

The most effective people on the face of the planet are not those with the best personal electronic devices; they are those who see themselves as serving others. They see what they do as a means of service. They find in what they do a means to serve others. They find energy, joy, and passion. It is in this sense that their thinking determines the outcome.

2. Reorder Your Priorities

The second step is to take an honest look at your life and its fabric, its spiritual center. Wayne Dyer tells us that the energy we focus on is what we bring into our lives.

I run a middle-school mentoring and tutoring program for at-risk kids who have no positive role models. I've described that program in the pages of this book. Certainly the kids and their families are beneficiaries of the program. But so also are the mentors and the tutors, active participants in the miracles that happen daily in the program. These are busy people—lawyers, doctors, engineers, professionals, and businesspeople—who find the time to serve.

The mentors and tutors are people like you and like me, with one difference: They do not allow themselves to be ruled by false priorities. How do I spend my time? What message am I sending to my children and to the world about what is truly important? "I don't have time for tutoring; I need to watch that program on television… With my work schedule, I can't get there and back…Wednesday afternoon is my tee time; I have sooo much to do." My friends, these are not simply excuses to avoid mentoring and tutoring. No, they are nothing short of excuses to avoid the meaning and indeed the joy in human life.

Perhaps you need to get out of the nursery; perhaps you need to get out of yourself and truly empty yourself of ego. The opportunities are many: A service club, twelfth-step work in a twelve-step program, pro bono work in a profession, success modeling in a mentoring and tutoring program…

Ask these questions, and answer them with honesty: How am I of service? How can I be of service? How can I reorder my priorities? In the 1991 movie *Regarding Henry*, based on a true story, Harrison Ford plays the role of a ruthless attorney whose life is changed in an instant, forcing him to reorder his priorities. Let's have a look at Henry's story:

> To everyone who knew him, Henry was a successful trial lawyer. In truth, he hated his job, but he worked hard at it anyway, and it consumed his time and energy. He worked constantly and was known as an excellent litigator—a trial lawyer willing and able to "take down almost anybody." Henry and his wife had one daughter, Jessica, who was ten years old. She attended a private boarding school two hundred miles from the family home.
>
> One late night, on the way home from the office, Henry stopped at a convenience store to pick up some cigarettes. As he was leaving the store, a young man with a gun held up the convenience store. In the chaos that ensued, Henry was shot in the head. He was gravely wounded but survived the gunshot. Because of the damage to his brain, Henry was forced to learn all over again how to speak and think. After nearly a year of painful and painstaking rehabilitation, he returned to work.

Henry still hated his job, but something had changed inside of him. He began to explore other vocations, and eventually he stopped practicing law. One day in the fall, he left the law office for the last time, went home to pick up his daughter's beloved dog, and drove two hundred miles to his daughter's boarding school. He and the dog found Jessica in a school assembly, where the school's headmistress was addressing the student body. Henry and Jessica, both in tears, hugged, while the dog jumped for joy on his two hind legs. "Henry," the headmistress said, "we're in a session here."

"I'm sorry to interrupt," Henry said, "but I've missed my daughter's first eleven years...I don't want to miss any more."

Henry and his daughter (and her canine best friend) went home together, where they met up with Henry's wife, Jessica's mother. That night, for the first time in years, they all shared a meal together. Henry never returned to the practice of law, and Jessica never returned to the boarding school.

Henry's story is unique in some ways. His priorities were reordered by a gunshot wound to the head. Through his experience, Henry found a new vocation he loved that was rewarding in every way. He took a management job in a major nonprofit, where he not only found his training as a lawyer useful, but also began to feel truly of service.

Through his change in thinking and priorities, Henry also found a huge release of love and compassion for his daughter and wife. Do you see? He began to serve. Thankfully, it does not require a gunshot wound to change our thinking and reorder our priorities.

Henry came to know that he needed a drastic reordering of priorities, and he acted on that. He came to know that the truest and purest form of service is boundless love in our own homes.

Like Henry, what have you missed in your life and the lives of those you love as a result of your thinking and your priorities? What can be different? What can you do to bring love and compassion to those you love most – and to those you encounter every day?

3. Seek Conscious Contact with a Power Greater than Yourself

Many of us have grown up with the conception that we can or should know all the answers, or at least that we as humans can discover the answers. We are taught that accepting something, anything, on faith becomes a sign of weakness. Nothing could be further from the truth. Part of the power of service is this: If you truly serve others, a power greater than yourself—by whatever name you choose to call that power—will indeed find you. And, if you choose to, you will find faith. Faith takes courage. Bengali artist Rabindranth Tagore said, "Faith is the bird that sings when the dawn is still dark." And faith is infinitely more difficult for the human mind and heart to embrace than is the absence of faith and the doubt and fear that accompany the faithless. In the movie Miracle on 34th Street, Kris Kringle tells the doubting single mother, "If you can't accept anything on faith, you are doomed to a life dominated by doubt."

If we truly knew who walks beside us at all times, we could never again experience fear and doubt. Never!

Right now, seek conscious contact with a power greater than yourself and ask Him or Her for help and guidance. If you feel so led, pray and meditate. As Peter Kreeft, author of Prayer: The Great Conversation reports, it has wisely been said that "no one who has ever experienced a higher power in prayer has ever found anything more joyful, not even owning half the world." Be still and listen... a power greater than yourself wants what's best for you, but you've got to want it too!

If a power greater than yourself, your Higher Power, stands at the door and knocks, open it. The question then becomes not "How can I serve?" but rather "How do I feel led to serve?" Service is not between you and me, or even between you and a friend. It is between you and a power greater than yourself. Perhaps you need to renew the creative side of you and touch the eternal in all of us with music, poetry, and great literature. Perhaps your verse includes bringing great joy—peace and beauty—to others through your creativity. The exciting thing is that when we reorder our thinking and our priorities, a power greater than ourselves opens many doors and shows us many avenues of service: Leadership in a food drive, creative writing shared with others, reading to a shut-in, sharing with a friend about things that matter. Or in simply, without condition, loving another...for it is in love and forgiveness that we truly serve.

Suddenly, we need not have all the answers. We are freed; available to serve as led, to love and forgive others as a power greater than ourselves has loved and forgives us. The power of service is unleashed in ourselves and in others.

American journalist Charles Kuralt told the story of a seventy-eight-year-old man he met in Virginia who was led to serve. The man bought land and paid for the building of a park that was available to all. In that park, along with other amenities, were picnic tables. Every year, the man would take vegetables grown in his own garden and leave them on the picnic tables for anyone who might want or need them. Kuralt asked the man, "Why do you do all of this?"

The man replied, "I knew it was what I was supposed to do at this time in my life. If you don't leave the world a better place than when you found it, what's the sense of your being here?"

Indeed.

Questions to Think About

■ Who is the happiest person you know? Does that person's energy, passion, and joy come from being of service to others? How does he or she serve others? How can you be more like that person?

_____

_____

_____

■ Do you see what you do every day as worthwhile and important, or do you see it as meaningless and worthless? If the latter, what can you do to reorder your thinking? Seeing yourself as being of service to others will lead you to greater joy.

_____

_____

_____

■ Are you willing to shift the paradigm of your thinking, to change what may be decades of thinking? Are you willing to live with the belief that everything you do is or can be a vessel for service—at home, at work, with neighbors? Are you willing to free yourself in this way to find deep meaning and great joy?

_____

_____

_____

■ What do you spend the hours in your days doing?
Those activities are your priorities. What message
does your involvement in those activities send to your
children and others around you? What kind of activities would align better with your higher purpose in
life? How can you reorder your priorities?

_____

_____

_____

■ Have you ever sought conscious contact with a power
greater than yourself and asked Him or Her for help
and guidance? Are you willing to give it a try? If so,
try it now, right where you are.

_____

_____

_____

Chapter 8

Serving through Love and Compassion—For Yourself and for Others

"It is in love, compassion, and forgiveness that we truly serve."
—Donald Clinebell

I've spoken in these pages about the need for a reordering of thinking, of the activity that goes on in the six inches between our ears. It is a change, a reordering, that for many of us requires a fundamental shift in the way we have thought and lived for decades. I encourage you to be patient and kind with yourself; it takes time to effect this change. This is a change in your thinking that you may never have contemplated. But if you stick with it, the rewards are many and rich, including empowerment to live with deep meaning and great joy.

Oscar Wilde once said that "to love oneself is the beginning of a lifelong romance." For some of us, our view of our own lives and our own selves has kept us in a very dark room. Some of us are fighting against ways of living and thinking that we learned well as children. We learned to believe that we have little or no control over much in our past and in our current lives. But what we come to learn over time is that we do have control over our own attitudes and our own thinking. And that it is not only okay; it is essential that we learn love and compassion for ourselves. Thoughts of judgment and self-loathing can be changed. They are not who we are. Over time, we come to learn and accept some fundamental truths about ourselves: "I am not perfect, but I am making progress. I serve my family, whom I love and adore just as they are, without condition. I do what I do as a servant, with a servant's heart. I live a life filled with love, compassion, and forgiveness—for me!"

If these truths seem strange at first, almost foreign, that means only that we have effectively cut ourselves off from our truth, from ourselves, and from the truth about ourselves. But as the shift occurs, this place of love, compassion, and truth yields extraordinary bounty. I am not a man who gets up in the morning and accomplishes nothing, hates his work, has nothing to offer to those I love or to the world. No! I am a source of goodness...of love, compassion, forgiveness, serenity, and peace. I am imperfect, but I am the creation of a power greater than myself. I am by nature a good man, filled with the capacity to love and forgive. You are all of these things, too!

The shift is difficult, but the rewards are immense and unlimited, powerful beyond measure. As your thinking shifts, you will be astounded at the opening of the floodgates...and the flow of love and compassion for your spouse, your children, and other human souls. Could it be that a shift in our thinking about ourselves creates a shift in our thinking about others? A shift in our thinking about family and those most precious to us. A love and compassion released in a deep and rich passion and joy.

It has been said that the truest and purest act of service is in loving another unconditionally, in love and compassion for others. Many never reach this place of true service because they are unwilling to look at themselves and at their thinking about themselves. As Carl Jung said, "Your vision will become clear only when you can look into your own heart." Those who sit in fear, self-doubt, and depression will not care for themselves or others. They will not serve others, and they will not find energy, passion, or joy.

To move to a new place of truth and strength takes courage. Sit with it. Make a beginning. Reread this chapter if necessary, concentrating on how it "feels."

Sit quietly with your children, with your spouse, with a person close to you. Be still and know that help and comfort are always available—in professional settings, in recovery settings, and in a loving power, a Higher Power greater than yourself.

Give yourself the gift of love and compassion. Love yourself as your Higher Power loves you, and watch what happens…at home, at work, in your life, and in the lives of those you touch.

Questions to Think About

■ Do you have any negative thoughts about yourself
that are sabotaging your joy and feelings of self-
worth? Where did these thoughts originate? From
your parents? A coach or teacher? An ex-spouse?
What can you do right now do to show yourself
more compassion and understanding? Doing so will
remove the obstacle to your becoming a loving family
member and valuable servant leader.

_____

_____

_____

■ To what extent do you love those closest to you
unconditionally? How can you do a better job of this,
removing your own expectations from the love you
give?

_____

_____

_____

Chapter 9

Think Differently, Do Differently

"Most men [and women] lead lives of quiet desperation.
And go to the grave with the song still in them."
—Henry David Thoreau

There are a lot of "yous" in this book. Largely because I've asked you to ask yourself some fundamental and difficult questions and to examine the service-driven life openly and honestly. Now it's time for some "I's," about how I came to reorder my thinking and my priorities in life. I want to share with you how I learned to think differently and do differently, in the process becoming empowered to live with meaning and joy I had never dared to imagine.

Think Differently

What goes on between my ears? In the mid-seventies, I graduated from law school. Top schools, top honors, and then nineteen years of schooling came to an end at the impossibly young age of twenty-six. I was a lawyer. I found myself in public service with The Legal Services Corporation, at that time a public corporation delivering, or at least attempting to deliver, legal services to those who couldn't afford lawyers. Then, almost before I warmed a chair at Legal Services, I moved on to the California Attorney General's office, a Deputy fighting for truth and justice and against oil companies. Wow, public service. And yet…

There are, just in the state in which I reside, more than 200,000 active and practicing lawyers. Most of them, or so say the polling data, are depressed, cynical, and unhappy. I was one of them. I found myself working at something I was very good at but I loathed. I disliked other lawyers, I disliked judges, I disliked the system—and I disliked myself. What I did for most of my waking hours was a means of financial security—nothing more. Was there a

God present in this? Did He care? Was I serving anyone but myself? Surely not, I thought.

Despite my thinking, I flourished in "the law." I sued oil companies and won; I was promptly promoted within the AG's office; and in the early 1980s, I moved to the big money in a large law firm. Four years later, I opened my own law practice. My unhappiness grew along with my income. The world seemed a bleak, self-serving place. I tried to find meaning in a marriage, then another. And I watched, almost from outside of myself, as happily ever after simply wasn't. There was the loss of a child through miscarriage and a failed marriage. I began to drink to excess. I had not yet found meaning in life, not even close.

Earlier in this book, we saw that understanding service and its power requires an answer to an all-important question. The powerful play goes on, and you may contribute a verse. What will your verse be? What will be the contribution of your life? Therein lies the joy, the energy, the passion!

For me, the reordering of my thinking did not come by lightning bolt; it came by quiet assurance. It came by a still, small voice. It came in moments of silence. It took work. I came to know my verse slowly, over time.

With the help of others, I began to see the very dark room I was confined in—by my thinking. I had come to know a way of living that was focused not on my loving servant's heart but on a very dark room—both literally and figuratively—in the back of the house where I resided. I began to see the need for love and compassion—first for me.

What followed was, for me, nothing short of miraculous. As my thinking about "me" changed, so did my thinking about others. I began to truly understand and act on that phrase I'd heard so many times: "unconditional love for others," especially for my family.

One day, as I sat watching my very young children play, I was moved toward something brand new, something from what I now know was a spiritual place I had never known. I felt a quiet assurance. At that moment, I allowed myself a thought that was indeed foreign: "I am worthy. I am good. I am loved. It's going to be okay."

I make a living for those most precious to me. I now do it with a servant's heart. In my profession, my vocation, I help others and serve others every day. I make others' lives better. Do I like everything about what I do daily in my profession? Of course not. But that's okay. I still serve, every day, and I find great meaning and joy in that.

Early in my career, I worked in the California Attorney General's "Environmental Enforcement Section." I was a Deputy Attorney General charged with suing oil companies for what were called "Reid Vapor Pressure" (RVP) violations at the gasoline pump. The results of elevated pressure at the pump are devastating to the environment, but the cost of lowering RVP is huge, and in some cases, the oil companies saw violations as worth the risk. I sued. I saw myself in some sense serving the "people of the state of California." Then one day a senior Deputy, an Assistant Attorney General, began settling or dismissing cases—strong cases, in my view—for no apparent reason. I saw oil companies settling major violations with "civil penalties" that seemed like petty cash—funds it seemed were taken from the CEO's sock drawer.

Some very dark thinking appeared in me: "What's the point? What I'm doing is useless and a fraud." But this was fundamentally misguided. Will every avenue of service produce immediate and successful results? Of course not. Does that make me less "of service?" Of course not. It is my thinking that either stymies or releases the power of service. It is within my control to find a servant mind and heart, to find in what I do a means to serve others, to see myself as serving others. And to understand that everything I do is, or can be, a vessel for service. My thinking determines the outcome.

Over time, I came to reorder my thinking, simply to change it in a way I had full control over. I began to focus on service to my family, within my chosen profession, and to neighbors and others. I also began to focus on my love of music as an avocation worthy of pursuit. For me, playing the piano is like breathing. I spent several decades not breathing. I began to play the piano every single day, to revel in it, to find again the joy in it, to share it with others who wanted to hear. I love to sing; ah, we're all singers at heart. I now choose to sing my song, both literally and in my thinking. I sing to the God of my understanding. And I share my singing, my song, with others who are moved by it. I love to write and to speak about my writing. I choose to share my gifts with others, to touch another life.

Do Differently

As I began to reorder decades of negative and controlling thinking, it was time to take an honest look at my priorities. I had to ask myself, "How am I of service? How can I be of service? What are my priorities?"

My new thinking began to move me head-first into new empowerment, new passion, new purpose...and into great joy. My relationship with my children blossomed and grew as I began to see, feel, and act out of love and compassion in my home and as I began to see what I do every day as a means of service. By finding a means to serve others, including my family, in what I do, I began to find true joy.

As love and compassion for myself and others grew, I began to look for and genuinely want opportunities for service in the practice of law, both pro bono and for services I am paid for. I signed up to be on a lawyers' committee serving pro bono seventy-two United Methodist Churches in the Orange County District of California. I also signed up to sing in a praise team at a church in town, although at the time, that's all I wanted to do there: sing! My profession, and leadership in it, led me to Rotary, the most accomplished service organization on the face of the planet. It is an organization in which leadership is about service. I was moved— no, led—to have a hand in training some 7,500 Rotary presidents during ten years of speaking and writing. I was moved—no, led— to found, and more important, to serve in the groundbreaking and multiple-award-winning 7th-Inning Stretch Middle School Mentoring and Tutoring Program for kids at risk. It is one of the most effective and honored mentoring and tutoring programs ever devised for at-risk kids, and now it serves as a model for school districts and service clubs around the world. I chose to let the God of my understanding draw near to me. And when He did, he led me to the meaning and joy of a service-driven life and the blessings of The Service-Driven Institute. For that, I remain grateful beyond measure.

Finding a Power Greater than Myself— The God of My Understanding

The God of my understanding never gave up on me. The places I found Him may surprise you. I found Him close at hand, knocking at the door. I found Him in prayer and in meditation. In the midst of my doubt, I prayed a simple prayer: "Help me. Please." Or just "thank you." In 1300 AD or so, German theologian Eckhart von Hochheim wrote, "If the only prayer you say in your whole life is 'thank you,' that would suffice."

I found Him in the eyes of my children and in their playful laugh on a summer afternoon. I found Him in His unconditional love for me and the unconditional love that began to pour out of me. I found Him in the moment of release from the pain and suffering of alcohol abuse. I found Him in the assurance that comes in a quiet moment. I found Him in the music I made at church. I found Him, in the end, in the eyes of those I served and serve. Where love and service were, God had been there all along.

I found Him in the eyes of a child in south Mexico who had never received a Christmas present till there was me. I found Him in the eyes of a child at risk, graduating with honors and as the first college-bound child ever in her family. I found Him in the eyes of those six million children walking the face of the planet polio-free. And I found Him in a mother's tears of joy at seeing her children for the first time ever.

And now, with the help of the God of my understanding, I serve, albeit imperfectly, my precious family, my friends, my "neighbors," perfect strangers, and those I will never know, in love and forgiveness. I serve kids who are at risk and in need of mentoring. I serve "neighbors" in the far corners of the earth, some whose names and faces I will never know. I plant shade trees under which I will never sit.

When I opened the door, the God of my understanding "supped" with me; he empowered me and led me to serve with joy, energy, and passion through my law practice, through Rotary, through AA, through Sunday School teaching, through my music and writing, through The Service-Driven Life book, through this book of Extraordinary Living, and through The Service-Driven Institute. I came to know true meaning, purpose, and great joy. And I came to understand that this God—the God of my understanding and a power infinitely greater than me—had been there with me the whole time. In a very real way, when I sought Him, He found me. And in that and in my story, I found enormous relief, peace, comfort, love, and a new-found freedom.

Will this be your experience? Perhaps not. It is indeed my story. Your story may be different. But if you stay open to a Higher Power, a Creator, a source, a power greater than yourself, you will thereby stay open to a spirituality filled with great meaning, with love and comfort and peace and joy. More on staying open to your spirituality in the following chapter.

Questions to Think About

■ How can you think differently to make a commitment to serving others in every part of your life?

_____

_____

_____

■ What can you do differently to begin living a service-driven life?

_____

_____

_____

■ Do you resist the ability of a Higher Power, the God of your own understanding, to provide you with guidance, comfort, and joy? Will you commit to being more open to this concept and phenomenon in your own life? There is power—and courage—in putting your faith in a power greater than yourself.

_____

_____

_____

■ What parts of the author's story in this chapter did
   you relate to? Why? Are there things you may want to
   do or change in your own life? Write those down, or
   enter them on your device—now.

   _____

   _____

   _____

Chapter 10

Embracing the Power of Service and the Service-Driven Life: An Extraordinary Life Awaits

"What we do for ourselves dies with us. What we do for others [through home and family, through vocation, through neighbor] is and remains immortal."
—Anonymous

T his book is not about easy answers to difficult questions. The service-driven life is not necessarily an easy life. It is, however, a life of great and profound meaning, power, and joy. It is by definition focused outside of ourselves and our egos. For many, it is counterintuitive to what we've been taught. But remember this: Statements like "I'm stuck," "I can't change," and "I don't have time to serve in my life and the lives of others" are off the table for good! They are nothing more than the ways of thinking that have kept you from experiencing meaning and joy.

Begin today, now. Take steps to accept a service-driven challenge you'll find on the Service-Driven Institute website. And understand this: The question of service is no longer a question. It is an answer filled with meaning, purpose, energy, hope, joy, and gladness. There is great joy in service.[1] We find ourselves with a passionate and powerful commitment to all that is good in ourselves and in others. The powerful play goes on, and you may contribute a verse! (Here I am referring to Walt Whitman's Leaves of Grass, O Me! O Life!) How exciting that is!

I encourage you to embrace now the power of service and find an extraordinary life in six specific ways.

1. Be Open to a Higher Power

"In music, in the sea, in a leaf, in an act of kindness
I see what people call God in all these things."
—Pablo Casals

---

1 . A. J. Russell, Ed., *God Calling* by Two Listeners (Pasadena, California: Hope Publishing House, 2012).

Be open to a power greater than yourself, in your service and in your life. As we discussed in the Preface of this book, spirituality is simply a sense of connection to something bigger than ourselves, to a higher purpose. It is part of a universal search for meaning. Notice that this description of spirituality refers to a "higher purpose," not a "Higher Power." Extraordinary living always includes a higher purpose; it may or may not include a Higher Power (God).

My personal belief is that at some level, whether conscious or not, every man and woman on the planet longs to know a Higher Power, a power greater than him or herself. If you have such a power in your life, may you now invoke the blessing, comfort, and presence of that faith—in your extraordinary life. If a faith base is not a part of your life, I understand. No preaching here. But stay open. A loving Creator, Source, Higher Power, a power greater than yourself is near if you call upon Him in truth.

Consider the case of Albert Einstein. Einstein, a brilliant man of science and rational thought, spent much time and energy exploring and writing about God and theology. He was a supremely rational and scientific mind, and in his early years, he was an avowed agnostic. Yet in seeking the truth of the cosmos and its construct, he found his way, or was led, to the God of his understanding. Einstein reached a fascinating conclusion and "religious" endpoint:

> The highest satisfaction of a scientific person is to come to the realization that God Himself could not have arranged these connections any other way than that which does exist.

We are in the position of a little child entering a huge library filled with books in many languages. The child knows someone must have written those books. It does not know how. It does not understand the languages in which they are written. The child dimly suspects a mysterious order in the arrangement of the books but doesn't know what it is. That, it seems to me, is the attitude of even the most intelligent human being toward God.

To sense that behind anything that can be experienced there is something that our minds cannot grasp, whose beauty and sublimity reaches us only indirectly. In this sense, I am a devoutly religious man.[1]

By seeking truth in science, and in the way the cosmos is constructed—in perfect "orderliness" and harmony—men and women of science often end up in "humility"—in the presence of a "magnificent structure that we can comprehend only very imperfectly," in the words of Albert Einstein. Ironically, such a scientific analysis in brilliant people who are able to recognize a perfect and ordered harmony in the cosmos has led many to a belief in a power greater than themselves—to a new spirituality.[2]

---

1 . Walter Isaacson, *Albert Einstein: His Life and Universe* (New York: Simon & Schuster, 2007), 385–7.

2 . For more on this topic, see Francis Collins, *The Language of God: A Scientist Presents Evidence for Belief* (New York: Simon and Schuster, 2006).

This book is not about the language of God, the power of science, or the power of God. Rather, it is about the power of service. This book is about what happens to us when we truly serve in every part of our lives and the power of service is unleashed. If you truly serve others, you may well feel a power greater than yourself moving in your life and heart. Be open to those miraculous moments of service. Remember, many believe that where love and service are, there is God. From my personal standpoint, the service-driven life is much enriched by a faith base.

If you sense the "meaningful coincidences" that Carl Jung talked about—events that have no apparent causal connection but are "meaningfully related"—a new, powerful, and comforting synchronicity may await you. Perhaps a spiritual awareness awaits you, along with the release of the extraordinary and life-changing power of service.

In any event, stay open to enlightenment, defined as the giving of spiritual light. Spirituality, in whatever form it manifests in you— in a Higher Power and thus a higher purpose, or simply in a higher purpose—is a blessing beyond measure.

2. Serve in Every Part of Your Life

We unleash the power of service when we truly understand that everything we do—yes, everything—is a vessel for service. Those who are truly service-driven learn to serve in every part of their lives: through home and family, through work and vocation, and through neighbor and others. In Chapter 1, we talked about the "Service-Driven Circle," as opposed to the "Me Circle." In the

Service-Driven Circle, service touches every part of our lives. The Service-Driven circle reminds us to make a conscious and intentional decision that everything we do is or can be a vessel for service. And in that circle is where the power of service resides. Let's look at service in each part of our lives. The website for The Service-Driven Institute contains three service-driven challenges—one with home and family, one with work and vocation, and one with neighbors and others.

The Truest Form of Service: Home and Family

As Mother Teresa taught, true service begins in the home. The first mission field is home and family. The truest and purest act of service is loving another unconditionally. Nowhere is that truth more visible and fulfilling than in the love and compassion released at home, in a deep and rich passion and joy. Embrace it! Imagine it! Strive to embrace fully the flow of love and compassion for your spouse, for your children, and for other human souls. What you do in your home and with your family can now be the truest and purest form of service, bringing love, compassion, forgiveness, and joy to all in your home. Let's look at some way to embrace the power of service in home and family.

Words can love, or words can hurt

What we say in our homes and to our family members matters. You may have heard children say, "Sticks and stones will break my bones, but words can never hurt me." As adults, we come to know that the notion that "words can't hurt" is fundamentally false. Words can hurt. Their use and misuse can set relationships back by years and can damage relationships almost irreparably, requiring enormous and, in a sense, "perfect" forgiveness. Ask a psychotherapist or psychiatrist engaged in marriage counseling how often he or she hears from a client about something hurtful the client's spouse said. Or ask a child therapist about hurtful words a parent said to a child. Such words often stay with us for years. If unaddressed, forgiveness and intimacy can become impossible.

Words can set back relationships for years, or they can take relationships to a new and joyous level of love and compassion. Use words to bless rather than harm those you love most. When necessary, practice forgiveness. Perfect love means perfect forgiveness. A lack of forgiveness is really a lack of love.

What we don't say matters as well. How long has it been since you spoke words of love and compassion, out loud, to those you love? Spend no time berating yourself if you have fallen short. Instead, act now, today, to change that. Take Service-Driven Challenge #1, below.

There is another way that what you don't say matters. There are times when saying nothing is the most loving thing you can do. Are you a person who has to be "right"? When you talk with the people or person most important to you, do you need to be right? Many people will sacrifice everything—serenity, peace, self, relationships—on the altar of "being right." That altar is a lonely place.

Try this. Just for today, try not having to be right. If you are engaged in discussion with one you love and you think you are right and feel compelled to tell that loved one that you are right, don't. Wait an hour, a day, or as long as it takes till the compunction—the obsession—to be right subsides. It will if you'll let it. But you must be willing. In the meantime, say nothing except, perhaps, "you [your loved one] may be right. Let me consider what you're saying." When the need to be right about the matter under discussion subsides or lessens, see how that feels. Less burdensome? Freeing? Loving? Compassionate?

The purpose of such an exercise is to help you choose love and compassion and to see how that feels. Choose love and compassion. Choose humility. When we use words in love and compassion, we can step aside and watch amazing things happen to the peace and serenity in our own lives, in our homes, and in the relationships we value most of all in this world. Choose love, compassion, and forgiveness daily, and by doing so, you will invite joy into your home!

There is another time when saying nothing is the most loving thing you can do. When you are feeling pain, hurt, or anger, and we all do from time to time, you must carefully screen and filter what you say to those you love. Everything that comes into our brains does not have to come out of our mouths. Perhaps what you are tempted to say comes not from a "clean" place of honest feeling, but rather from feelings that are all about you and have nothing to do with those you love. In these moments, say nothing. Are you a person who tends toward sarcasm? If so, don't. The word "sarcasm" comes from the Latin word sarcasmos and the Greek word sarkasmos, meaning "to tear flesh; sharp utterance designed to give pain." Ow! Do not use your tongue to hurt others, to tear flesh. When in doubt, say nothing. Speak later, after taking a hard look at the underlying feelings. Words can love, or words can hurt. You make the choice. By so doing, you are introducing into your home the truest form of love and service. Joy will not be far behind.

Be a force for love and forgiveness in your home

Here's another way to think about embracing the power of service in home and family. As we've seen, love and forgiveness are powerful forces; where they are practiced, relationships blossom and grow, and joy comes in the morning. Where there is love and forgiveness, there is the God of your understanding, a power greater than yourself. What a spectacular concept!

Be a constant in times of calm, contentment, serenity, and prosperity and, perhaps more important, in times of pain, suffering, sorrow, addiction, loneliness, and conflict. Yes, it is difficult to love and forgive in times of pain, conflict, and stress. But when we do, we find a power greater than ourselves; perhaps a God of our understanding was present the whole time. The transformation in home and family is both astonishing and miraculous. And it's available to all who embrace the truest form of service.

Remember Henry

We talked about Henry's story in an earlier chapter. Remember him to help you embrace service in home and family. Henry said, "I missed my daughter's first eleven years. I don't want to miss any more." Like Henry, what have you missed in your life and the lives of those you love—as a result of your thinking and your priorities? Write about that, if you feel so inclined. Seeing your thoughts on paper or on one of your devices is often very helpful.

If you've fallen short, accept that and forgive yourself. Okay, so you've fallen short. But you are also a person who is willing to look at yourself and ask yourself some difficult questions. And you are willing to do the work to grow and progress—to learn to embrace meaning, purpose, and joy in your life and thus in the lives of others. Were that not true, you would have put this book down long ago. Accept that you have fallen short, make amends where necessary… then forgive. Until you forgive yourself, you cannot and will not move forward.

In thinking about and remembering Henry, think about your life as if you've been given a new chance to live in a new and exciting way. And that is exactly what you have before you! What does that mean for you? What can be different? What can you do to bring love and compassion, and a little peace and serenity, to your home and to those dear ones you love most of all? Service-Driven Challenge #1 is a good place to begin:

Take Three Service-Driven Challenges

You may say, "Okay, I see that service is the common thread of meaning in our lives on this planet, and I am moved by the extraordinary, but anecdotal, stories of service and great joy, but how do I know that service is the key for me?" I have a challenge for you—no,

I have three challenges for you. If you want to see service at work in your life, if you want to step outside of yourself and find meaning and joy in your own life, empowered in service, take the service-driven challenges below. They won't take large blocks of time, they don't cost money, and they will affect every part of your life with the key to a life that matters, that makes a difference.

The first challenge applies to your home and family, the second applies to your vocation and work, and the third applies to your neighbors and others.

Service-Driven Challenge #1—
Service in Your Home, with Your Family

Mother Teresa reminded us that "true service begins in the home." Imagine your home filled with love, compassion, and "perfect" forgiveness. Then do the following:

1. Think differently. Sit quietly. Close your eyes.
   Imagine the floodgates opening up—floodgates
   of boundless love, compassion, and transforming
   forgiveness. Joy and peace will not be far behind!
   Think of everything you do in your home and with
   your family as a vessel for service.

2. Do differently. Deliberately. Have a meal with your
   family. Have two meals with your family. Have
   another. And watch relationships grow and bloom,
   in good or bad times. Sit down with your spouse or

significant other. Talk with him or her. Truly listen. Love. Forgive.

3. Watch what happens. Joy and peace will not be long in coming. Write about it; write to us about it (theservicedrivenlife@gmail.com). Talk to others about it, in your home and outside of it. (Consider using the Member blog through www.theservice-drivenlife.org.) You may well be amazed at the release of love, compassion, and forgiveness in your own life and in the lives of those most precious to you!

Service-Driven Challenge #2—Service through Work and Vocation

Let's look at some ways to embrace the power of service in vocation. There are several.

1. Examine what you do and how you do it. What goes on between your ears about your work? Do you think of yourself as worthy? Do you think of yourself as good at what you do? Do you look for the good in what you do?

Find in your profession/work the good in what you do and how you do it and the ways in which you make others' lives better. Do it now. Do you like everything about what you do daily in your vocation? Perhaps not. Despite that, serve others!

Will every avenue of service produce immediate and successful results? Of course not. Does that make me less "of service?" Of course not. It is my thinking that either stymies or releases the power of service. It is within my control to find a servant mind and heart, to find a means to serve others in what I do, and see myself as serving others, and to understand that everything I do is or can be a vessel for service. My thinking determines the outcome.

2. Identify how you are of service through your work and vocation. Know that you serve others through your vocation, through your work. It's already happening! A lawyer helps her client through a time of great difficulty; a gardener creates beauty in the lives of those who see his or her work; a pastor offers the congregant/parishioner a place of calm in the midst of a storm, a life-changing and life-saving place of calm and peace. What about the utility worker who brings to hundreds of thousands of people the electric power necessary to their lives? Or the teacher who offers his students not just knowl-edge and learning, but role and success modeling? The employer who provides jobs and thereby makes the lives of his employees and their families better? The employees who make the employer's business a success, create jobs for more employees, and multiply productivity?

Think of a server in a fast-food restaurant who offers the customer food, but also adds a friendly tone and a warm smile. The customer, taken aback, says, "Thank you…for making my day a little better." In that moment, in that corner of the globe, the worker is very much of service. It is a moment of power and of meaning. This kind of moment can happen and does happen every day, in every profession and business, in every vocation.

3. Decide how you can be of service through your vocation. Write about the following questions: How do I now serve through vocation? Who is helped by what I do? Be kind to yourself. Do not judge or punish yourself. See the good in what you do. Stay open to the possibility that a power greater than yourself wants you exactly where you are in vocation. Then move on to this: How would I like to serve through my vocation? What can I change in my thinking, and my actions, in my vocation? What more can I give pro bono to others in what I do, and to whom?

A lawyer I know is an estate planner. He makes it a regular part of his week to visit no-charge clients and former clients who are now confined to skilled nursing homes. First on his list are seniors who have no one who can or will visit. Frequently, this lawyer shares a meal with those he visits, complete with nursing-home cuisine. To a place often filled with loneliness and pain, he brings a great gift. He eases the pain of many. And he is changed. He is renewed.

4. Allow yourself to be newly empowered in your vocation. At the beginning of this book, I talked about empowerment, about learning to live outside of ourselves and thereby finding deep meaning and great joy for ourselves—being empowered in service to others. This fundamental truth is no less true in our vocations.

Also earlier in this book, I asked you to imagine a world in which service comes first—men and women living in service to others in every part of their lives. And so it is with vocation.

Imagine what would happen if you brought into your workplace the meaning you've discovered, the power and joy that are now yours. What would happen to your work and your work product if you thought of yourself as worthy? And if you saw yourself as fundamentally good, as loving and compassionate, filled with the capacity to forgive? If you thought of yourself as good at what you do? If you looked for the good in what you do? If you saw yourself as being "of service" in your work? As you begin to see yourself as "of service" to clients, customers, students, and patients, you will bring into your life a new energy, peace, and contentment.

Perhaps most important, as you see yourself in vocational service to your family, you will embrace a fundamental truth about what you do and how you serve. In your vocation, you support those most precious to you. That support can be an enormously loving gift. Do what you do in vocation with a servant's heart. If you allow yourself that much—to love and serve your family in vocation—you will begin to experience a very welcome peace and contentment in that part of your life. With acceptance of yourself and what you do in vocation, the floodgates will open. Not only will you experience new peace and contentment; you will find new energy, passion, and productivity in your work. This change in your own attitude and thinking is a very powerful concept. It is the power of service.

Consider this story about vocation involving a man and his daughter:

> A young dad was reading to his six-year-old daughter as she was going to sleep. The dad paused and a far-away look came over him. His daughter noticed. "What's wrong, Daddy?" she asked.
>
> "Oh, nothing," the dad said. "It's Sunday night, and tomorrow's Monday."
>
> "Daddy, you like Friday better than Monday, huh?"

"Yes, I do. I don't like my work much."

The daughter thought about that for a minute, then said, "Daddy, I like Monday better than Friday. On Mondays I get to go back to school and talk to my friends, and I get to learn cool things."

"You know, sweetie, you're really something. Thank you for that."

Wisdom from a six-year-old? Indeed. A six-year-old who knows at some level that life does not happen strictly outside of vocation, outside of the way in which we spend 80 percent of our time, outside of the way we spend the substance of our days. She has learned, even at six, that vocation is a part of life; she knows at some level that she has a part in a greater work. She has not been created for naught!

But the young dad is not alone, is he? You've seen the studies out there that tell us that 70 percent of men and women in the work-force hate how they spend their days. They dread going to work, feel they accomplish nothing, see what they do as meaningless and worthless, and feel "actively disengaged" from what they do in their vocations.

When on Sunday night the young dad thinks about Monday morning, he feels powerless and without joy, meaning, or hope. Consider this: How would the young dad's life be different if he discovered a way to change his thinking?

What would happen to Dad if he truly saw everything he does—everything—as a vessel for service, including Monday morning and the way he spends the substance of his days?

If we choose—and it is a choice—to live in misery in our vocations, we are choosing to live 80 to 90 percent of our lives without, or outside of, the power of service, outside the meaning and the joy of service that we can embrace and live every single day!

How can we make a different choice? Let's take Service-Driven Challenge #2:

1. Think about your work, the way in which you spend the substance of your days. Then think of it this way:
   "[A power greater than myself]
   has created me to do
   Him some definite service;
   He has committed some work
   to me which He has not
   committed to another. I have
   my mission—I have a
   part in His great work; I am a
   link in a chain, a bond of
   connection between persons.
   He has not created me for naught."
   —Cardinal John Henry Newman (1801–90)

2. Say out loud, "A power greater than myself—by whatever name I call that power—has not created me

for naught!" Say this every day for a week, with your morning coffee or meditation, or both, and say it again before you go to bed each night.

3. Experience the meaning, empowerment, and joy that will begin to accompany you to and in your place of vocation.

4. If you want to take further steps in service through vocation, have a look at pages 87 through 91 of The Service-Driven Life book; there you will find six ways to discover your path of service through vocation.

Service-Driven Challenge # 3—Service to Neighbors and Others

"A man or woman has made at least a start on discovering
the meaning of human life when he plants shade trees
under which he knows full well he will never sit."
—Elton Trueblood, American Quaker Theologian

Service to "others," through neighbors and as a neighbor, is, in a sense, the classic "service." It is what most of us talk about when we talk about service, sometimes in the biblical context ("love your neighbor as yourself" and "what you do to the least of these, you do unto me") and sometimes in a secular context ("do unto others as you would have done to you").

What you will find as you embrace the power of service is that you have moved into an extraordinary life; a life filled with new energy, passion, purpose, and joy. Service is no longer a question. It is who you are—a man or woman of love, compassion, and forgiveness with an irrepressible call to serve others. We are learning to live outside of ourselves and moving toward those we love most dearly, toward those we work with, and toward our neighbors, both literally and figuratively. We seek opportunities to serve. The opportunities are limitless. (See Appendix 1 to this book, a great place to find the path of service uniquely yours in service to your neighbors.)

Here are some suggestions to help you embrace the power of service to your neighbors:

1. Take action! Make a first step. Make contact. Make a call to a mentoring program for kids at risk, to the food bank in your community with empty shelves, to the home for seniors looking for readers and performing artists. Make a call or send an e-mail to the service organization you've thought about for years but have never seriously pursued. Perhaps you are drawn to the service club whose members build clean water pumps and tanks in India and other countries around the globe or the service organization working toward the eradication of the wild polio virus that is now active in just one country on the face of the planet.

2. Commit now. Commit an hour or two to a project that attracts you. If you need help with projects

available to you in your community, see the list of
organizations that need volunteers in Appendix 1.

3. Watch and write about what happens. Write about it.
Write to us about it. And remember, where service is,
so also are meaning, empowerment, and great joy—
in those served and in those who serve! Experience it
now!

The key to this challenge is that first step: Take action. Watch out
for that thinking that separates us from meaning and joy: "I don't
have time." "If only…" "Nothing I do is worthy." That thinking
and those responses are off the table! For good. Now be open to the
amazing places—literally and figuratively—you will be led to!

In serving others through neighbors nearby and across the
globe, think about tapping your creative side, a side of you that
may well have been dormant for many years. Perhaps your service
includes bringing great peace, joy, and beauty to others through
your creativity as you touch the eternal in all of us—through music,
poetry, or great literature. Play the piano at a retirement home filled
with seniors who would love to hear you play. Read to that senior
who can no longer read on her own, the one who thinks all have
forgotten her.

Be open to serving in ways that may never have occurred to
you before. I know a very good and successful lawyer. He is also
a juggler. He rides a unicycle and juggles at the same time. He has
an "act" that is very "unlawyerlike" and very funny. It would be

stand-up comedy if the juggler wasn't sitting down on a unicycle during the act. He performs his act mostly for family. One day, this lawyer-juggler was invited to take his act to a local retirement home. The lawyer-juggler wasn't sure about it. Why would anybody want to see him do his act? But he did it. He unicycled and juggled for a hundred seniors, complete with a wonderful stream of commentary and jokes. The lawyer- juggler had a ball, and so did the crowd! They smiled, roared, and cheered. And cheered some more. For those moments in time, the lawyer-juggler brought great joy to a place that is not always joyful. To a place filled with stories of loneliness and pain, he brought a great gift of love and service to his neighbors. He was changed; he was renewed.

Look inside for what is within you, for the gifts you've been given—gifts with which you are uniquely equipped to love and serve. Those gifts are there in each of us. Trust in them. Know the power, the simplicity, and the joy of service.

3. Spend Some Time Reading the Avenues of Service in Appendix 1

In embracing the power of service to others, you may wish to spend some time in Appendix 1, a powerful resource in itself. Think about the many programs and projects described there. You may be amazed at the many programs and projects that need volunteers. You may be amazed at the power and joy you find traveling along these "avenues." From food banks to mentoring, to "surfers healing" to therapeutic riding of horses, and from low-cost housing projects to the adoption of kids no one wanted into loving homes. These are the stories of servants serving neighbors, not as conqueror or boss, nor as victim or trampled rug. Rather, these are stories of humble servants bringing to those they serve love, compassion, and great joy. They are servants finding for themselves a joy without measure.

They are servants learning to live outside of themselves, thereby finding deep meaning and great joy for themselves, empowered in service to others. Servants who know that service is not an add-on to life but that service is the core and foundation of worthiness, fulfillment, meaning, empowerment, and great joy! Imagine!

4. Spend Some Time with the Stories of Service in Previous Chapters and Appendix 2

Throughout this book are stories of service that are filled will inspiration and meaning, power and joy. You'll find stories of service in Chapter 4 and also in Appendix 2. You may wish to reread all of these stories of service. Here is a sampling, to remind you about a story that may have moved you deeply:

- The blind mother and the surgeon

- Janet and the food drive

- Henry and the power of changed thinking and priorities

- The stories of mentoring and the great joy in those served and those serving. "Can there be any doubt that through my service I am changed?" the mentor asked.

■ The stories of Josh and Kevin

Perhaps one of the stories in the text of the chapters caught your attention and moved you deeply. There is power in "story," in the pictures we see of others who serve. At the end of selfless service are changed lives. Read the stories again, slowly this time, perhaps writing down what draws you to a particular story. Do you see the power of service in the story? Changed lives? Servants living extraordinary lives because they have learned to live outside of themselves? Servants as diverse as Einstein, Schweitzer, Mother Teresa, and Gandhi who have learned that the only person with any chance of happiness is the person who finds a way to serve?

5. Be Extraordinary—Take Action

I have a couple of concrete suggestions to give you an immediate start in embracing the power of service and the service-driven life.

1. Write in a journal. Write about your service. Start with a writing tablet, a spiral notebook, or simply three sheets of paper. Or use your computer or tablet. Create for yourself a path-of-service journal. At the top of the first page, write "Serving through Home and Family." At the top of the second page, write

"Serving through Vocation," and on the third page, "Serving through Neighbors."

Over the next several days, or even weeks, keep your journal with you; write as you feel called to write. Don't worry about style, grammar, syntax, or how much you are writing. Just write as moved. Add what you find yourself thinking about, ways in which you now serve and things you would like to do differently. How would you like to serve? How do you feel moved to serve? And where? Sit with it. Enjoy the process. Take your time.

Be kind to yourself. It has been said that the highest form of wisdom is kindness. That includes kindness to yourself! Each of us must give ourselves the gift of love and compassion. Perhaps for you that means loving yourself as does that power greater than yourself—unconditionally and fully. Now is the time to feel that gift, to feel love and compassion for yourself. Not tomorrow, but now.

Think and feel about what it says about you that you are truly willing to examine yourself honestly, that you truly seek to grow spiritually and in values-based principles. That you are willing to work to make your life truly extraordinary. By this very commitment, you are already extraordinary! This is an exciting time for you.

2. Take action today. Even if it feels like a small action to you, remember that no gift is poor if it expresses the true love of the giver. Start down a different road, a different avenue, than the one you've been traveling. Go outside of yourself now. Move toward the extraordinary. Move toward the light.

The moment of action you spend today may be life changing, for you and for another human soul. Smile at the homeless person outside the convenience store. You know the one—the one you've avoided eye contact with for weeks or months. Give him your pocket change. Or engage him. Direct him to a local church or other resource where he can connect with a local food bank or family assistance ministry. Or better yet, connect him yourself with such a place of love and compassion. Feel the power and the meaning of who you are and what you are doing, with yourself and with others.

A young woman approached me after a lecture I once gave the week before Christmas in a large hotel. While attending the lecture, the woman had been feeling depressed and lonely about the Christmas season. During the lecture, she said, she had felt a shift in herself about the season and she "knew"—"almost as if somebody had put the thought in my mind"—that she needed to do something different. Here's what she did: She took that small sum of money she had set aside for Christmas spending and gave it—wholly, deliberately, and intentionally—to an organization seeking funds to provide clean water to children who have none.

This young woman's decision seemed to her at the time a small gesture, a small act. But the impact of her decision on her was both immediate and profound. The woman was led to become a volunteer in the organization she had contributed her Christmas funds to, and she is now a key player in the fight to bring clean water to every child on the face of the planet. She has never forgotten the "knowing"—the spiritual growth she felt on that day at Christmas time.

What does this story tell us? Two things. First, when you feel moved to act in service, act. Whether at home, at work, or with a neighbor, act! Even if it seems a small act or gesture. The young woman in the story took action; she began with a financial donation. There is service in that. But that was only the beginning. As her path of service became clear to her, this woman of service came to know that it was the gift of herself that truly changed her life and the lives of others. Second, when you feel a spiritual move in your life—whether it's a power greater than yourself, the God of your understanding, or neither—go with it. Come alive in it. Advance confidently, knowing that when you serve, you have invoked a powerful truth in your life and in the universe. What is that powerful truth? Only the foundation and core of worthiness, fulfillment, meaning, empowerment, and great joy.

In the service-driven life, we live and love powerfully. We imagine and bring to fruition a world in which service comes first, in every part of our lives. C. S. Lewis reminds us that often we live in the shadowlands. "The sun is always shining somewhere else; around the bend in the road, over the brow of the hill." When will we realize that this is our time? This is our time to recognize the power of service and to serve and love. As Mother Teresa said, "let us begin." If nothing else, take a step to unleash the power; begin in your own home. Or be concrete and intentional with neighbors and others: Choose not to contribute to the $450 billion that Americans spend each year on Christmas presents.[1] Rather, contribute deliberately and with a true servant's heart to the $10 billion needed to provide clean water to every child on the face of the planet. The impact on the children without clean water will take time. The impact on you will be immediate and profound.

And then…make that call to the mentoring program for kids at risk, to the food bank, to the home for seniors. The opportunities are only as limited as our thinking and our willingness to serve.

Tap your creative side and see what your source, your Higher Power, the God of your understanding moves in you. Change your thinking. Change your priorities. Then go inside for what is within you, to serve and to love. It is there, in each of us. Trust it.

Philosopher Martin Buber said it this way: "We cannot escape the compulsion to acquire things and power…so let us, cautious in diction, mighty in contradiction…love…powerfully."

---

1 . *Orange County Register*, December 30, 2006, part 2, page 2.

Our presence in the lives of those we love and serve…without strings, without expectation of return—that is loving powerfully. Love powerfully, and you will make a difference, miraculously, in the lives of those you serve…and in your own life. The deliberate and intentional choice to live a service-driven life will be life-changing and will empower you to live with deep meaning and great joy. "So that your joy may be complete."

6. Embrace the Power of Service and Live Service-Driven, Intentionally and Deliberately, Every Day

Stay focused on those powerful words: "service-driven." Remember that being service-driven, putting empowerment in service, is at the core of worthiness, fulfillment, meaning, and joy. Make a deliberate and intentional choice to align what is important in the way you live your life—the core value of service—with your spirituality—that is, with your life's higher purpose, something bigger than yourself. And remember, no one can tell you your life's higher purpose; that is for you to discern, guided by your belief system (see Chapter 3) and its foundational values. Your higher purpose may include a higher power, a God, faith, or no faith. One thing is certain. If your values include the common thread—the foundational value—of service, your higher purpose must include being of service, in every part of your life.

It is only in this way that you will discover a peace beyond understanding, a sense that your life has deep meaning and fulfills a larger purpose. My friend, the "hidden power" that answers life's most compelling question is no longer hidden. The power of service creates extraordinary lives, rich with fulfillment and worthiness and steeped in meaning, purpose, and great joy, beyond all imagining.

Imagine yourself filled with love, compassion, and forgiveness; imagine yourself service-driven. Imagine a world filled with people just like you. Consider joining The Service-Driven Institute. There are many benefits of membership, at no cost or obligation.

Participate in the blog on the Institute's website, engaging with other service-driven men and women. Spend time with the service-driven meditations designed to keep you on the service-driven track. And remember this: "Your power to help others lives will soon bring its delight, even when, at first, the help to yourselves may seem too late to bring you joy."[1]

An American proverb says that "before sunlight can shine through a window, the blinds must be raised." In seeking to live with purpose and meaning, we are often our own worst enemies because of the way we think. Does it seem too late? Too much work? Too much change? If you cannot change your thinking yet, come out of your head and focus on your center, on your heart, and see how it feels. Do one thing today, anonymously, that will make someone else's life better—in your home, at work, and in the world of others.

Most of all, do not underestimate the power of service. If it seems counterintuitive, go with it till it feels intuitive. Do it till you truly believe that only those among us who seek and find how to serve, in every part of our lives, will ever be truly happy.

---

1 . Russell and Sand, *God Calling*.

Samuel Beckett (1906–89), an Irish playwright and novelist, wrote a now-famous play called Waiting for Godot. Throughout the length of the two-act play, the two main characters, Vladimir and Estragon, are waiting for someone (or something) named Godot. The reader never learns who Godot is; we learn only in the end that he or she never shows up. Beckett's themes often dealt with suffering in human life, and Waiting for Godot has been viewed as a reflection of Beckett's existentialist view of life. That is, people are searching to find meaning in life, and to find out who and what they are throughout life, as they make choices based on their experience, beliefs, and outlook.

This exchange between Vladimir and Estragon is revealing:

"Let's go."

"We can't."

"Why not?"

"We're waiting for Godot."

Most of the play deals with the fact that the protagonists are waiting endlessly for something that never shows up.

Are you waiting for Godot? Do you feel a void, a lack of meaning and purpose? A lack of joy in your existence? Wherever you are on your life's journey, know this: If you are waiting for happiness, peace, and a life that matters, that makes a difference, it will not show up unless you do something about it. In the words of Vladimir, "Let's go."

Make a choice to embrace the power of service and the service-driven life. Be open to a Higher Power of your understanding. Choose to serve in every part of your life—yes, every part—at home, at work, and with neighbors, both literal and beyond. Live a service-driven life intentionally and deliberately, every single day. And watch as your life is no longer about waiting for something that never seems to show up. Watch as your life becomes truly extraordinary.

In the service-driven life, we find the key to an extraordinary life, a life that matters, that makes a difference. In the service-driven life, we find ourselves empowered to live with great joy, with purpose and meaning, with energy and passion—with hope, strength, and love. And with a new sense of our own spirituality. That is what it means to embrace the power of service. That is what it means to embrace the service-driven life. And that is what it means to be fully alive!

> "Yesterday is gone. Tomorrow has not yet come.
> We have only today. Let us begin…"
> —Mother Teresa

Questions to Think About

■ In times of difficulty, to what extent can your family and colleagues depend on you to be the voice of reason and calmness? What can you do to become more of a constant in such times?

_____

_____

_____

■ Do you have trouble forgiving others? Is lack of forgiveness preventing you from moving past a situation you experienced with someone else? Do you see that the lack of forgiveness hurts only you? Are you willing to forgive that person now, as an act of love for yourself, a way of increasing the energy of love and service in your life and on the planet? It is you who will benefit, you who will be unburdened, you who will find a new freedom.

_____

_____

_____

■ Do you have a creative side that has been squelched over the years? How can you use your creativity to serve those around you? What is something specific you can do to use that talent to bring joy to someone else?

_____

_____

_____

■ Have you ever kept a journal? Are you willing to begin a "path-of-service" journal? Identify ways you can serve through your home and family, your work and vocation, and your neighbors (both local and worldwide).

_____

_____

_____

■ Will you commit to joining, at no charge or obligation, The Service-Driven Institute? (www.servicedriven-institute.com) Will you share your story and your journey with other members and others striving to live service-driven lives?

_____

_____

_____

■ Will you take the three Service-Driven Challenges in
this chapter? Will you write about your experiences
with those challenges?

_____

_____

_____

Appendix 1

Avenues of Service

No endorsement of any charity or organization listed is expressed or implied.

There is great meaning in the pages that follow; there is great power and great joy here. Travel down these avenues now, and spend some time considering how others serve, changing the lives of those they touch and their own lives!

If, as you travel these avenues of service, one or more of the projects or programs described tugs at your heart, check the "take action" box to the bottom right after the project/program description. When you've finished this book, you can come back to the "take action" boxes you've checked.

Remember, it is important to commit, to take that first step outside of oneself, in service to neighbor (and in service in home and family and at work). Commit in writing, on a personal digital device, or with another person. Commit to think differently and do differently. Then take action—be extraordinary! The moment of action you spend today may be life changing, for you and for another human soul.

Acres of Love
www.acresoflove.org/

Acres of Love is a legally registered South African nonprofit organization, which owns and operates homes for abandoned infants and children, providing a noninstitutional setting and pristine environment for the infants and children rescued and entrusted into our care. Infants and children live and thrive in de facto families.

❑   Be extraordinary. Take action today.

American Dental Association International Dental
Volunteer Association
http://internationalvolunteer.ada.org/

On this website, you can browse or search over 100 organizations offering volunteer opportunities around the world. This site is a starting point for international service opportunities in the dental field. Do your research before undertaking any project! Also contains information on how to put together your own project.

❑   Be extraordinary. Take action today.

American Medical Association Volunteer Opportunities for Physicians
http://www.ama-assn.org/ama/pub/about-ama/our-people/member-groups-sections/office-international-medicine/volunteer-opportunities-for-physicians.page

General resources on Physician volunteerism.

❏   Be extraordinary. Take action today.

Big Brothers Big Sisters of America
www.bbbs.org/site/c.9iLI3NGKhK6F/b.5962345/k.E123/Volunteer_to_start_something.htm

For more than one hundred years, Big Brothers Big Sisters has operated under the belief that inherent in every child is the ability to succeed and thrive in life. As the nation's largest donor and volunteer supported mentoring network, Big Brothers Big Sisters makes meaningful, monitored matches between adult volunteers ("Bigs") and Children ("Littles"), ages six through eighteen, in communities across the country.

Being a Big Brother or Big Sister is one of the most enjoyable things you'll ever do. Not to mention one of the most fulfilling. You have the opportunity to help shape a child's future for the better by empowering him or her to achieve. And the best part is it's actually a lot of fun. You and your Little can share the kinds of activities you already like to do.

Play sports together. Go on a hike. Read books. Eat a pizza with extra anchovies. Or just give some advice and inspiration. Whatever it is you enjoy, odds are you'll enjoy it even more with your Little— and you'll be making a life-changing impact.

❑   Be extraordinary. Take action today.

Boys & Girls Clubs
www.bcga.org

In every community, boys and girls are left to find their own recreation and companionship in the streets. An increasing number of children are at home with no adult care or supervision. Young people need to know that someone cares about them.

Boys & Girls Clubs offer that and more. Club programs and services promote and enhance the development of boys and girls by instilling a sense of competence, usefulness, belonging, and influence. Boys & Girls Clubs are a safe place to learn and grow—all while having fun. It is the place where great futures are started each and every day.

❑   Be extraordinary. Take action today.

Boy and Girls Clubs of South Coast Area Tutoring Program
http://www.bgcsca.org/programs.html

Like this Boys and Girls Club in California, many such Clubs have active and successful volunteer tutoring programs for kids at risk, struggling in school, or both. Contact your local Boys and Girls Club to learn more about how to apply and requirements for participation.

❑   Be extraordinary. Take action today.

Boy Scouts of America
www.scouting.org/Volunteer.aspx

The Boy Scouts of America relies on dedicated volunteers to promote its mission of preparing young people to make ethical and moral choices over their lifetime by instilling in them the values of the Scout Oath and Scout Law. Today, nearly 1.2 million adults provide leadership and mentoring to Cub Scouts, Boy Scouts, and Venturers.

Through the dedication of these many volunteers, the Boy Scouts of America remains the foremost youth program of character development and values-based leadership training in America.

To these volunteers, Boy Scouts of America say thank you for your dedication to Scouting.

And, to adults who are not currently Scout volunteers, you are invited to become a volunteer and share in the positive experiences of Scouting programs.

❏   Be extraordinary. Take action today.

Bread for the World
www.bread.org

Bread for the World urges the nation's decision makers to end hunger at home and abroad. These men and women help neighbors, whether they live in the next house, the next state, or the next continent. Confronting the problem of hunger can seem overwhelming. What can one person do? Plenty. Bread for the World members write personal letters and e-mails and meet with members of Congress.

Working through churches, campuses, and other organizations, Bread for the World engages more people in advocacy. Each year, Break for the World invites churches across the country to take up a nationwide Offering of Letters to Congress on an issue that is important to hungry and poor people.

❏   Be extraordinary. Take action today

The Clinebell Institute
http://theclinebellinstitute.org

The mission of The Clinebell Institute is to offer the community a commitment to serve the whole person by offering professional, affordable pastoral counseling and psychotherapy, educational opportunities for personal growth, and training for pastoral counselors.

Pastoral counseling uses the insights and principles of spirituality, religion, theology, and modern behavioral sciences in working with individuals, couples, families, groups, and institutions toward the achievement of wholeness and health. An important dimension in pastoral counseling different from other approaches to counseling and psychotherapy is the conviction that mental and emotional health is best understood when spiritual, religious, and psychological needs of individuals are addressed.

For more information, see the website of the American Association of Pastoral Counselors, www.aspc.org.

❑ Be extraordinary. Take action today.

Coastal Mountain Youth Academy
www.cmya.org

Coastal Mountain Youth Academy provides an educational and therapeutic setting for adolescents who have struggled in a traditional school environment. It's a community with a sense of teamwork that stands to solve the problems associated with addiction, abuse, harassment, and self-harm. CMYA's programs offer a safe, nurturing, blame-free environment that enables students to achieve their full potential.

❑ Be extraordinary. Take action today.

Doctors Without Borders
http://www.doctorswithoutborders.org/

"Medical aid where it is needed most. Independent. Neutral. Impartial."

❑ Be extraordinary. Take action today.

Exchange Club
www.nationalexchangeclub.org

Founded in 1911 in Detroit by businessmen who wanted to "exchange" ideas, the Exchange Club moved its headquarters to Toledo in 1917. For nearly one hundred years, its volunteer efforts have supported the needs of the country and of local communities, making it the country's oldest American service organization operating exclusively in this country.

❑   Be extraordinary. Take action today.

Faith Based Service

There are many extraordinary avenues of service through faith based churches, including but not limited to the major religions and their denominations, and non-denominational churches. Many faiths have extensive service projects and programs around the corner, and around the world.

If your belief system is based in faith, you may wish to consider the many service opportunities there. Several world-wide churches fund foundations and organizations that are "first on the ground" when disaster strikes, anywhere in the world.

If you want to find this way to serve, be in touch with your pastor, or priest, or minister or rabbi, or other church or faith leader.

❑   Be extraordinary. Take action today.

Family Assistance Ministries
www.family-assistance.org

The South Orange County Family Assistance Ministries was founded in 1999 to continue to accommodate the families the Episcopal Service Alliance could no longer serve. The first case, in September 1999, provided rental assistance to an individual so eviction could be prevented. Within thirty days, this individual became employed at a major retailer and became self-sufficient and a productive member of the community.

Now, Family Assistance Ministries is providing temporary assistance to more than six hundred families and individuals.

❑   Be extraordinary. Take action today.

Feeding America Food Bank
http://feedingamerica.org/take-action/volunteer.aspx

Feeding America Food Bank members help provide low-income individuals and families with the fuel to survive and even thrive. As the nation's leading domestic hunger-relief charity, this network supplies food to more than thirty-seven million Americans each year, including fourteen million children and three million seniors.

How the Network Works

Feeding America benefits from the unique relationship between its 202 local member food banks at the front lines of hunger relief and the central efforts of its national office.

Each day, hunger is experienced in every community across this country. In fact, this network feeds more than thirty-seven million neighbors each year. Ending hunger in American depends on the volunteer work of literally millions of Americans who know that they can make a difference.

There are as many different ways to volunteer as there are individuals and communities across this country. You can help out in your local community through activities such as:

Tutoring kids at your local kids' café

Repackaging donated food for use by food pantries

Transporting food to charitable agencies

Doing clerical work at the national office

It's simple—get involved today, and get your family and friends involved. To find opportunities in your area, please contact your local food bank which can be found through the network's website.

❑   Be extraordinary. Take action today.

Feed My Sheep
http://feedmysheepgulfport.org/category/volunteer/

Feed My Sheep is a nonjudgmental, faith-based program dedicated to providing nourishment to the homeless, homebound, and needy of the Gulfport area. Service is provided on a "no questions asked" basis.

How to get involved:

Deliver meals through a local church

Donate to and help support this mission financially.

Volunteer your time and touch a life.

There are many ways to get involved. Visit Feed My Sheep online—including the website or on Facebook or Twitter for volunteer and event updates.

❏   Be extraordinary. Take action today.

General Federation of Women's Clubs
http://www.gfwc.org/

The General Federation of Women's Clubs is an international women's organization dedicated to community improvement by enhancing the lives of others through volunteer service. Collectively, we are Living the Volunteer Spirit.

❏   Be extraordinary. Take action today.

Girl Scouts of America
www.girlscouts.org/for_adults/volunteering/

Be a Girl Scout volunteer!

What did you do today? As a Girl Scout volunteer, you'll add meaningful days to girls' lives and to your own. Tackle everything from global warming to election reform. Travel to incredible places.

Share your personal passions and create experiences together you'll never forget.

Schedule tight? No problem. There are endless, flexible ways to participate.

Since 1912, Girl Scouts has built girls of "courage, confidence, and character, who make the world a better place." Girl Scout volunteers are a diverse group of women and men whose expertise, skills, interests, and life experiences nurture each girl's individuality and leadership qualities.

❏   Be extraordinary. Take action today.

Global Dental Relief
http://globaldentalrelief.org/international-volunteer-opportunities/

International opportunities for service for dental hygienists and staff and dentists. Projects in Africa, India, Asia, Central America.

❏   Be extraordinary. Take action today.

Goodwill Industries International, Inc.
www.goodwill.org

Goodwill Industries International enhances the dignity and quality of life of individuals, families and communities by eliminating barriers to opportunity and helping people in need reach their fullest potential through the power of work.

For more than a century, volunteers have advanced Goodwill's ability to improve lives, families, and communities. Goodwill recognizes that in order to fulfill its mission, it needs the help and support of those in local communities.

Each of the 165 local Goodwill organizations is led by a board of volunteer leaders who help shape their organization's work to meet the needs of their community. Valued volunteers contribute their time, knowledge, and support in a variety of ways.

❏　　Be extraordinary. Take action today.

Habitat for Humanity
www.habitat.org

Habitat for Humanity is a nonprofit, ecumenical ministry founded on the conviction that every man, woman, and child should have a decent, safe and affordable place to live. Building with people in need, regardless of race or religion. Welcoming volunteers and supporters from all backgrounds. Former U.S. President

Jimmy Carter and his wife Rosalynn are Habitat's most famous supporters. The couple annually leads the Jimmy and Rosalynn Carter Work Project.

❑   Be extraordinary. Take action today.

Invisible Children
www.invisiblechildren.com

Invisible Children (IC) uses the power of media to inspire young people to help end the longest running war in Africa. The model has proven effective, and hundreds of thousands of people have been called to action through IC films and the volunteers that tour them.

IC is made up of a tireless staff, hundreds of full time volunteers, and thousands of students and supporters. They are young; they are citizens of the world; and they are artists, activists, and entrepreneurs. They are using their voices to ask the U.S. to spearhead efforts to bring peace to Northern Uganda. They are mobilizing a generation to capture the attention of the international community and make a stand for justice in the wake of genocide.

❑   Be extraordinary. Take action today.

Key Club
www.keyclub.org/discover.aspx

Key Club is an international student-led organization which provides its members with opportunities to provide service, build character, and develop leadership.

Key Club International is the oldest and largest service program for high school students. It teaches leadership through service to others. Members of the Kiwanis International family, Key Club members build themselves as they build their schools and communities.

❑   Be extraordinary. Take action today.

Kiwanis International
www.kiwanis.org

Kiwanis International is a global organization of members of every age who are dedicated to changing the world, one child and one community at a time.

❑   Be extraordinary. Take action today.

LA Food Bank
www.lafoodbank.org

Without volunteers, the Food Bank would not be able to provide food for thousands of hungry people every week. Get together with a social, church, or work group, and spend a day with the LA Food Bank. To learn more about becoming a Food Bank volunteer, contact the volunteer coordinator at (323) 234-3030.

❑   Be extraordinary. Take action today.

Laura's House
www.laurashouse.org

The mission of Laura's House is as follows: Changing social beliefs, attitudes, and the behaviors that perpetuate domestic violence while creating a safe space in which to empower individuals and families affected by abuse.

For any nonprofit organization, volunteerism is essential. Laura's House depends on volunteers to keep all of its programs running smoothly and consistently.

Fingerprinting is required for all volunteers and TB Tests for volunteers who work with children. All volunteers must complete the 40-Hour Training to work at the Counseling and Resource

Center or the Shelter. If you have particular skills in areas that you think could benefit Laura's House, please contact the organization.

❑　　Be extraordinary. Take action today.

Lions Club
www.lionsclub.org

Lions meet the needs of local communities and the world. The 1.35 million members of this volunteer organization in 206 countries and geographic areas are different in many ways, but share a core belief—community is what we make it.

❑　　Be extraordinary. Take action today.

Mary Erickson Community Housing
www.maryerickson.org

Mary Erickson Community Housing (MECH) is a 501(c) (3) nonprofit corporation and designated Community Housing Development Organization serving Southern California. Formed in 1991, MECH owns and operates affordable rental housing in Orange, Riverside, and San Bernardino counties. In addition,

MECH rehabilitates and develops single-family homes to provide home-ownership opportunities to income-qualifying households.

❑   Be extraordinary. Take action today.

Meals on Wheels
www.mowaa.org/

The Meals on Wheels Association of America (MOWAA) is the oldest and largest national organization composed of and representing local, community-based Senior Nutrition Programs in all fifty US states, as well as the US Territories. These local programs are the MOWAA members.

There are some five thousand local Senior Nutrition Programs in the United States. These programs provide well over one million meals to seniors who need them each day. Some programs serve meals at congregate locations like senior centers, some programs deliver meals directly to the homes of seniors whose mobility is limited, and many programs provide both services.

❑   Be extraordinary. Take action today.

Project Hopeful
www.projecthopeful.org

Project Hopeful invites you to join in spreading the truth about HIV/AIDS and children living with the disease. Help fight social stigma; join the Truth Pandemic.

❑   Be extraordinary. Take action today.

Rancho Sordo Mudo
http://ranchsordomudo.org

Rancho Sordo Mudo (RSM) is a free home and school for deaf children in Baja California, Mexico. Ed and Margaret Everett, the founders of RSM, believed that deaf children should be taught how to read and write, to communicate in sign language, and to learn a trade for their future. This has been the work of the ranch for more than forty years. Throughout the year, service groups and churches visit RSM, bring needed food and gifts for the kids, and spend time with the kids.

❑   Be extraordinary. Take action today.

Relay for Life/American Cancer Society
www.relayforlife.org/relay/newtorelay

Relay for Life is the signature fundraising event of the American Cancer Society. There are many components that make up a Relay for Life event, and there are many ways in which you can volunteer and participate in this special event.

To be involved with Relay for Life, you can be a Team Captain or Team Member, a Committee Member, you might be a Survivor or a Caregiver, or you might be an event sponsor, an "Event Day Volunteer," or a donor.

Regardless of your participation, the best way to learn more about how to become involved in your local community is to speak to someone in your local Relay for Life. This webpage provides you with some background information on Relay for Life, how to get involved, and where to turn for resources.

❏   Be extraordinary. Take action today.

Rotary International
www.rotary.org

Rotary. Humanity in motion.

Devotion to service above self: the excitement, the energy, the vision, the achievement. 1.2 million Rotarians, in the words of Martin Buber, "loving powerfully," changing lives; 1.2 million men and women across the face of the planet with something truly extraordinary in common. It's an organization of leaders committed to service in your community, in our nation, and in our world, making a difference every single day. Not seeking recognition for past projects, but looking for the next project through which to make a difference in the lives of those in need, of those who hurt. Dividing their service among community service, vocational service, international service, club service.

Rotarians host youth programs, senior programs, food and toy drives, health-related programs, projects to end polio, projects to bring clean water to every child on the planet.

Rotary videos

You can eradicate polio. You can promote peace. You can feed the hungry. You can help children do better in school. Because you can get involved with Rotary. Learn more at rotary.org.
www.vimeo.com/rotary

"Come join us"
www.vimeo.com/17540224

"This is Rotary"
www.youtube.com/watch?v=6vVyG0TJBWM

Rotary Programs

1. End Polio Now (www.rotary.org)—After twenty-five
   years of hard work, Rotary and its partners are on
   the brink of eradicating the wild polio virus from the
   face of the planet. But a strong push is needed now to
   root it out once and for all. It is a window of opportunity of historic proportions.

   ❑   Be extraordinary. Take action today.

2. Shelterbox (www.shelterbox.org)—Shelterbox is an
   international disaster-relief charity that delivers emer-
   gency shelter, warmth, and dignity to people affected
   by disaster worldwide. Volunteers are crucial to the
   work of Shelterbox. Without them, "we would not be
   able to function."

   ❑   Be extraordinary. Take action today.

3. Interact (www.rotary.org)—Interact is Rotary
   International's service club for young people ages 12
   to 18. Interact Clubs are sponsored by individual

Rotary clubs which provide support and guidance, but they are self-governing and self-supporting.

❑   Be extraordinary. Take action today.

4. Roteract (www.rotaract.org)—Rotaract is a Rotary-sponsored service club for young men and women ages eighteen to thirty. Rotaract clubs are either community- or university-based, and they're sponsored by a local Rotary club. This makes them true "partners in service" and key members of the family of Rotary.

❑   Be extraordinary. Take action today.

5. Rotary Youth Leadership Awards Camp (http://ryla5320.org/)—Rotary Youth Leadership Awards (RYLA) are all about Rotarians working with youth in leadership development. This is an intensive training/experiential program for 280 high school students in their pivotal junior year who are chosen for their proven or potential leadership abilities.

Students participate in an all-expense paid camp, help in Idyllwild Pines, California, for three days. The camp is organized by Rotarians and facilitated by RYL student Alumni. Students are joined by talented young people from communities throughout the district. RYLA provides a memorable opportunity to learn, grow, have fun, make new friends, and gain a new and improved focus.

What does RYLA offer? The core curriculum for RYLA includes the following:

What Rotary is and what it does for the local and international community

The importance of communication skills in effective leadership

Fundamentals of leadership

Ethics of positive leadership

Building self-confidence and self-esteem

Problem solving and conflict management

Elements of community and global citizenship

❑   Be extraordinary. Take action today.

6. The 7th-Inning Stretch Program—The 7th-Inning Stretch program for kids at risk provides mentoring and tutoring for middle school students and beyond…to rave reviews—and always heart-warming, sometimes miraculous stories. The core of the program, its mentors and tutors—role models, success models. Rotarians willing to be amazed at how little time it takes to set a new course in a child's life. Rotarians giving their time—an hour per week or more. Giving the gift of time and self that changes lives. Men and women choosing to make a difference in the lives of kids at risk.

Bottom line, the program succeeds because the kids are inspired by Rotarians. The parents and caregivers are inspired by Rotarians—men and women of success, in life and career, men and women of commitment, character, responsibility and…of service. Yes, the kids are inspired, but they cannot be inspired if they do not know you.

Past Rotary International President Frank Devlyn said this: "From Seattle to Santiago…from Bogatá to Bombay and everywhere in between, the children of the world are waiting. They are the hope of the future but we—you and I—are their hope that the future will be bright."

The 7th-Inning Stretch. Community service that changes lives—the lives of the kids, the lives of parents and caregivers, and yes, the lives of those who serve—the mentors and tutors.

For more information about the 7th-Inning Stretch Program, contact Donald Clinebell at theservice-drivenlife@gmail.com.

❑   Be extraordinary. Take action today.

Santa Barbara Rape Crisis Center
www.sbrapecrisiscenter.org/05Volunteer/volunteer.html

Volunteers serve as a vital support network, providing more than 20,000 hours of service to the community each year.

Crisis intervention advocacy requires sixty hours of training plus a one-year commitment to the Hotline. Training is held twice a year in English and once a year in Spanish. Female advocates cover a weekly six-hour shift on the twenty-four-hour Hotline and provide crisis counseling, information, advocacy, and accompaniment to survivors of sexual assault and their families and friends. Male and teen advocates also provide support to survivors and their loved ones and serve as educators on our Speaker's Bureau.

❑   Be extraordinary. Take action today.

Save the Children
www.savethechildren.org/site/c.8rKLIXMGIpl4E/
b.6540957/k.7CF9/Volunteer_Opportunities.
htm?msource=wexgghp1010

Save the Children is a leading independent organization for children in need with programs in more than 120 countries, including the United States. It aims to inspire breakthroughs in the way the world treats children and to achieve immediate and lasting change in their lives by improving their health, education, and economic opportunities. In times of acute crisis, Save the Children mobilizes rapid assistance to help children recover from the effects of war, conflict, and natural disasters. In 2010, the organization improved the lives of more than 64 million children in need in the United States and around the world. Save the Children invests in childhood – every day, in times of crisis and for the future. In the United States and around the world, Save the Children gives children a healthy start, the opportunity to learn and protection from harm. Save the Children welcomes and encourages committed individuals to apply as volunteers. Volunteer opportunities range from short-term to long-term assignments. They are offered in a variety of areas including, but not limited to, finance, fundraising, marketing and communications, public policy, and social media, as well as research and administrative work.

Volunteers for Save the Children educate, advocate, and fundraise for the organization from either the Westport, Connecticut, or Washington, DC, office.

US Volunteer Program

Save the Children highly values the myriad of contributions their volunteers make daily. A number of volunteer opportunities are available in the Westport, Connecticut, and Washington, DC, offices for individuals looking to make a difference in the lives of children worldwide. Save the Children welcomes and encourages committed individuals to apply as volunteers within all levels of our organization. Volunteer opportunities range from short-term to long-term assignments. They are offered in a variety of areas including, but not limited to, finance, fund-raising, marketing and communications, public policy, and social media, as well as research and administrative work.

To match your skills, abilities, and interests to the needs of Save the Children, you are invited to submit an application for consideration. A volunteer coordinator will contact you with options for getting involved.

❏　　Be extraordinary. Take action today.

Second Harvest Food Bank
http://feedoc.org/HowToHelp/DONATETIME.aspx

Volunteers bring their hearts and their hands to their work at Second Harvest Food Bank. Your work is vital to the mission of alleviating hunger in the community.

One of the most important ways you can get involved in Second Harvest Food Bank is by becoming a hunger relief advocate. Learn more on the Second Harvest website.

❏   Be extraordinary. Take action today.

Shea Therapeutic Riding Center
www.sheacenter.org

The J. F. Shea Therapeutic Riding Center is dedicated to improving the lives of people with disabilities through therapeutic horse-related programs.

Volunteers give their time, energy, and support to those in need. They have no expectations but are rewarded by the smiles and exultations of accomplishment from the clients they serve. As part of the Shea Center team, they serve from the heart. Would you like to be a Shea Center volunteer?

❏   Be extraordinary. Take action today.

Surfers Healing
www.surfershealing.org

Surfers Healing was founded by Israel and Danielle Paskowitz. Their son, Isaiah, was diagnosed with autism at age three. Like many autistic children, he often suffered from sensory overload—simple sensations could overwhelm him. The ocean was the one place where he seemed to find respite.

A former competitive surfer, Israel hit on an idea—with Isaiah on the front of his surfboard and Izzy steering from the back, the two spent the day surfing together. Surfing had a profound impact on Isaiah. Israel and Danielle decided they wanted to share this unique therapy with other autistic children. They began to host day camps at the beach, where autistic children and their families could be exposed to a completely new experience of surfing.

❑   Be extraordinary. Take action today.

San Clemente Jr. Woman's Club
http://www.scjwc.org/

For 68 years, the San Clemente Junior Woman's Club (SCJWC) has served the community with women committed to promoting volunteerism, improving the community, and fostering new friendships. SCJWC volunteers time and talent and provides financial support for civic, cultural, education and social projects.

❑ Be extraordinary. Take action today.

The Association of Junior Leagues, International
http://www.ajli.org/

The Junior League is a charitable, not-for-profit organization of women who make sustainable improvements in their communities as a result of the civic leadership training and expertise they obtain through their experience in the League.

Today, The Association of Junior Leagues International, Inc. is comprised of more than 150,000 women in 291 Junior Leagues throughout Canada, Mexico, the U.K. and the U.S.

❑ Be extraordinary. Take action today.

P.E.O International
http://www.peointernational.org/

Women helping women reach for the stars. Philanthropic organization where women celebrate the advancement of women, educate women through scholarships, grants, awards, loans and stewardship.

❏   Be extraordinary. Take action today.

The Smart Program Mentoring and Tutoring
https://www.thesmartprogram.org/volunteer

The Smart Program's flagship volunteer program, where volunteers are matched one-on-one with individual middle school students to help foster deep and meaningful relationships. Tutors commit to one evening per week. Mentors commit to spending time with their student at least twice per month.

In order to be considered for a position as a SMART mentor, you must:

- Be at least 21 years old

- Submit a completed volunteer application form

- Have an interview with a member of the SMART staff

- Submit to a criminal background check

❏   Be extraordinary. Take action today.

Water for Life
http://www.waterforlife.org/about

Water for Life uses a combination of appropriate water technologies, water health education and basic research so that communities can identify and solve their water problems. Its mission is not simply to provide safe water to those in need, but to train individuals and communities to create and maintain their own local water resources. Water for Life does so by a highly interactive process combining formal instruction with hands-on training.

Water for Life operates with an all volunteer staff, many of whom raise their own support as well as the finances needed to complete their projects.

❑   Be extraordinary. Take action today.

World Vision
www.worldvision.org

World Vision is a Christian humanitarian organization dedicated to working with children, families, and their communities worldwide to reach their full potential by tackling the causes of poverty and injustice.

Who They Serve

World Vision serves close to one hundred million people in nearly one hundred countries around the world. World Vision serves all people, regardless of religion, race, ethnicity, or gender.

Activities and Volunteering

Take the opportunity to share your time and talents in a meaningful way by volunteering at a World Vision office near you—an interactive, walk-through exhibit will transport you into the heart of Africa and the life of a child.

❑   Be extraordinary. Take action today.

YMCA Triangle Tutoring and Mentoring
https://www.ymcatriangle.org/programs-services/tutoring-mentoring

Many YMCA's fund mentoring and tutoring programs for kids struggling at school. This program is in North Carolina. But contact your local YMCA for information about volunteer programs, and the requirements for participation.

❑   Be extraordinary. Take action today!

4-H National Mentoring Program
http://www.4-h.org/grows/

The 4-H National Mentoring Program features replication of three Programs of Distinction, recognized for implementing effective mentoring strategies with goals of improving family relationships, increasing social competencies, increasing school attendance, reducing juvenile delinquency, youth unemployment, and school failure.

❑   Be extraordinary. Take action today.

Appendix 2

More Stories of Service; Empowered to Live with Meaning and Joy

The Story of Peter the Mentor

Peter was a real estate broker who was a Rotarian, a member of a local Rotary Club. Every Thursday afternoon, Peter participated in a Rotary-sponsored middle school mentoring and tutoring program for kids at risk. Every week Peter was at the school, where he mentored two students. These students were very much at-risk and in need.

One day, Peter came to me and told me that he was going through a work-related transition and was having some financial difficulties and could no longer be a Rotarian. With a tear in his eye, Peter continued, "May I continue to mentor and tutor, even though I'm not a Rotarian?

"Yes, you bet," I said. "That's what the kids need. You're a great asset to the program. And besides, we tutors and mentors will get to see you regularly too."

"Thank you," Peter said. And he started to leave the room. I hesitated.

"Peter," I called out as he reached the door. "You've got a lot on your plate right now, my friend. You can take a break if you need to."

Peter paused, turned around—the tear in his eye was now on his cheek—and said simply, "No, I need this. It is a place of great joy in my life." Indeed!

Yes, in service, great joy is built in. There is joy for those served and great joy for those who serve. Love and compassion and joy abide.

The Joy of Peer Mentoring

Rotary Youth Leadership Awards (RYLA) are set up so that Rotarians work together with youth in leadership development, but it is also about youth working with youth. In the end, RYLA encourages peers to mentor other kids.

My son, Brennan Clinebell, attended RYLA during his junior year of high school and returned to RYLA as an alumnus and peer mentor in his senior year. Here is how he describes the experience: "My name is Brennan. I love music and sports and have a passion for service. I am driven by my community and inspired by those around me to make this world better. The reason I returned to RYLA in my senior year was to give back and to spread the lessons it teaches people at my school and in my community. RYLA showed me that it's okay to be myself and to be proud of it. RYLA opened me up to new people and brought me out of my shell. It started me on a road that taught me that service is a core value, not an add-on, and a source of great joy."

Adopting HIV-Positive Kids

Countless children in Ethiopia and throughout the third world are born HIV-positive and lose their parents to AIDS. The sentence for these innocent kids: To live orphaned in Ethiopia in unthinkable poverty, with an early death sentence.

A married couple, Kiel and Carolyn Twietmeyer, were living in the United States with seven birth children. They adopted into their US home six Ethiopian children and founded Project Hopeful. Within a few years, the project was placing in loving US homes thousands of HIV-positive children from many different countries and is advocating everything on behalf of such kids.

Talk about extraordinary lives! The Twietmeyers have time and again written about the place of service at the center of their lives and about the gift not only of meaning and purpose, but of great joy. Their lives have become "richly fulfilled" in service through Project Hopeful.[1]

---

1 . Kiel and Carolyn Twietmeyer, on Hour of Power. www.projecthopeful. org

Appendix 3

Mission Statement of The Service-Driven Institute

Please visit the website of The Service-Driven Institute. Here is the organization's mission statement:

> Service isn't an add-on to life. Instead, it's the core and foundation of worthiness, fulfillment, meaning, empowerment and great joy. It's what we're made for.
>
> The Service-Driven^{SM} Institute was created to foster personal growth and fulfillment, to inspire men and women to be in service to and with others and to imagine and encourage men and women not to be served but to serve.
>
> The Service-Driven^{SM} Institute seeks to imagine and foster a world in which service comes first—a world filled with men and women living in service to others, in every part of their lives: through home and family, vocation and neighbor. A world filled with people learning to live outside themselves and thereby finding deep meaning and great joy for themselves, empowered by service to others.

The true measure of a man or woman has nothing to do with status. Life is not about prestige; it is about passion and purpose. It is about impacting the lives of others and understanding that everything you do—yes, everything—is, or can be, a vessel for service.

The Story Behind This Book

I have been a lifelong Methodist and "preacher's kid." I am the youngest son of Howard Clinebell, PhD, and Charlotte Ellen, PhD, one of three children. My father was an ordained Methodist minister for nearly sixty years, Professor of Pastoral Counseling at the Claremont School of Theology for nearly thirty-five years, a world-renowned author, a pioneer in the pastoral care and counseling movement, and a founding president of the American Association of Pastoral Counselors (AAPC). My mother is a psychotherapist who works with sexual assault survivors; she will leave a lasting legacy of strength, wisdom, and inspiration in that field. She has also written extensively on the relationship between the sexes and about working with children.

"What a family DNA," you might be thinking. And you are right.

As you will see when you read Extraordinary Living, the book is a product of my own life experience. It is also a product of a simple but profound conversation with my father in the fall of 2004. It was the last year of my father's life. I sat at his bedside, as I did many nights in those last days. As I sat, I helped Dad with his supper. And I shared with him that I believed I was meant to write a book. I had never written a book, although I considered myself a writer. I described to him a book about a life: a life centered around, and driven by, service. A life lived in service…in home and family, vocation, and in service to "neighbor." A story of renewal—from despair to hope, from darkness to light, from doubt to faith, from sadness to great joy! My father listened attentively, nodding gently, but did not speak. As we finished supper, we sat together in the quiet.

After supper, the gloaming turned to dark, and I read to Dad from a favorite daily reader. Sleep seemed next, and I prepared to depart for the night. But as I turned to go, Dad stirred and waved at me to return to his bedside. I sat. He smiled at me and said this: "Donald, you must write that book." He turned onto his side and he slept—a sleep he would later describe as restful and peaceful. I left, and I too spent a restful and peaceful night.

It was that night that I came to know I would one day write this book—Extraordinary Living: The Hidden Power That Answers Life's Most Compelling Question.

About the Author

Donald Clinebell, JD, PBK, is the founder and president of The Service-Driven Institute, whose mission is to imagine and foster a world filled with men and women living in service to others, in every part of their lives—through home and family, vocation, and neighbors. Service-driven people live outside of themselves and thereby discover deep meaning and great joy for themselves.

Donald is a popular speaker and published author. His first book, The Service-Driven Life, was released in January 2013 to rave reviews and the written endorsements of many in the fields of spiritual growth and wholeness, spirituality, and theology. The book is a powerful and moving exploration of the power of service in our lives—using Christian terminology and teaching. Extraordinary Living, released in 2016, is the follow-up to The Service-Driven Life. Extraordinary Living is a groundbreaking study of the power of service in all of our lives, using values-based spirituality.

A Rotarian for more than twenty years, Donald has been a frequent speaker and has helped train more than seven thousand incoming Rotary presidents worldwide. Rotary is the largest and most accomplished service organization in the world. Donald is founder and chair of the 7th-Inning Stretch Middle School

Mentoring and Tutoring Program for kids at risk. It is a community-service initiative that truly changes the lives of kids, parents/caregivers, and members/tutors.

Donald was one of five individual finalists nationally for the President of the United States National Community Service Award. He is a member of Phi Beta Kappa, a recipient of the Mary Ford Beacon Prize in Government, and a lifetime member of CSF.

He holds a bachelor of arts degree from Pomona College, magna cum laude, and a Juris Doctor degree from UCLA School of Law. He graduated with highest honors from UCLA's Trial Advocacy Program. From 1978 through 1984, he served as Deputy Attorney General for the California Department of Justice under Gov. Jerry Brown and Gov. George Deukmejian.

Donald is the founding and managing partner of The Clinebell Law Firm in San Clemente and Santa Ana, California. As volunteer counsel to several districts of the United Methodist Church and a member of the Annual Conference Lawyers Committee, he has represented more than fifty local churches pro bono.

A much-in-demand keynote and motivational speaker and lecturer, Donald speaks on topics including service, mentoring and tutoring kids at risk, the power of service, and the meaning and joy of the service-driven life. He is a UMC-certified lay preacher. The Service-Driven Life lecture/sermon series has taken him all over the United States and soon will take him to South Korea and Europe.

Raised in Claremont, California, Donald is one of three children born to Dr. Howard Clinebell, a founding faculty member at the Claremont School of Theology and a pioneer in the field of pastoral

care and counseling, and Dr. Charlotte Ellen, an icon in crisis counseling and women's issues. He is the proud father of two grown children, Brennan and Tessa. He lives with Bonnie in San Clemente,
California.

For more information or to order Donald's materials, contact him
at theservicedrivenlife@gmail.com or visit www.servicedriveninsti-
tute.com. To book Donald as a speaker, please visit www.service-
driveninstitute.com/resources/.

In Donald's words: "Service is no longer a question. It is who
I am. I strive mightily to '...live as a servant, and thereby I am
changed' (Mother Teresa)."

Donald's avenues of service include:

- Through home & family

- Through the practice of law, The Clinebell Law Firm

- Through writing and speaking

Volunteer counsel to the Orange County District of
 the United Methodist Church and a member of the
 Annual Conference Lawyers Committee, representing
 pro bono some 50 churches.

Charter member of the San Clemente Sunrise Rotary
 Club (SCSRC). Donald served as President of the
 Club in 1995-96. During his tenure, the SCSRC

grew in membership by a full 75% and won seven
District-wide awards and two international awards.

Assistant Governor, District 5320, Rotary International.
Mr. Clinebell is a frequent keynote speaker at Rotary
events.

Featured speaker and trainer at Presidents Elect Training
Seminar (PETS)—annual training seminar for
incoming Rotary Presidents. In that capacity, Mr.
Clinebell has had a major hand in training nearly
8,000 Rotary Presidents.

Founding Chair of the 7th-Inning Stretch Middle
School Mentoring & Tutoring Program for kids at
risk. Founded in 1995, the program has touched the
lives of thousands of kids. Community service that
truly changes lives—the lives of the students, of the
parents/caregivers, and the lives of the mentors and
tutors. The program has received multiple awards,
including the California Golden Bell, a statewide
award recognizing excellence in community-based
school programs. To learn more about the program,
please visit http://articles.ocregister.com/2006-03-17/
cities/24776692_1_rotarians-program-rotary-inter-
national.

Member of the San Clemente Dons, a service organization whose membership is made up of honored and
respected civic leaders.

Multiple Paul Harris Fellow and Paul Harris Society
Member (recognizing contributions to the Rotary
International Foundation, which Foundation has
funded over two billion polio vaccines since 1987).

Praise Team (vocal) member: Palisades United
Methodist Church & St. Andrews by the Sea United
Methodist Church. Our Saviors Lutheran Church.
Sunday school teacher, Third through Fifth grades.

Donald's scholastic awards include membership in Phi Beta
Kappa, the Mary Ford Bacon Prize in Government, Pomona College
Scholar, Life Member, California Scholastic Federation, Biography:
Who's Who in California.

More in Donald's Own Words

"I am so richly blessed, in so many ways—through home and
family, those most precious in my life, through "neighbors," those
whose path I have crossed and will cross. In vocation, I am also
truly blessed. I have been given a great gift: The opportunity to serve
others through the law and the legal profession.

And now, I have been given the opportunity to serve others with
the message of The Service-Driven ™ Life and Extraordinary Living.

May you be truly blessed and empowered by the deep meaning and great joy of Extraordinary Living!"

IF YOU'RE A FAN OF THIS BOOK, PLEASE TELL OTHERS

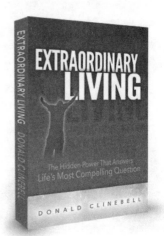

- Write about it on your blog and on Twitter and on your Facebook and LinkedIn pages.

- Suggest it to friends.

- When you're in a bookstore, ask them if they carry the book. The book is available through all major distributors, so any bookstore that does not have it can easily order it.

- Write a positive review on www.amazon.com.

- Send my publisher, HigherLife Publishing (media@ahigherlife.com), suggestions about websites, conferences, and events you know of where this book could be offered.

- Purchase additional copies to give away as gifts.

- Join the Service-Driven Institute: www.servicedriveninstitute.com

CONTACT ME

To learn more, feel free to contact the author at:

Donald Clinebell, J.D., PBK

servicedriveninstitute.com

theservicedrivenlife@gmail.com

Connect on social media:

Become a member at servicedriveninstitute.com

"Like" on Facebook at facebook.com/donald.clinebell

Follow on Twitter @DonaldClinebell

You may also contact my publisher directly:

HigherLife Publishing

PO Box 623307

Oviedo, FL 32762

Email: info@ahigherlife.com

Lecture Series

INVITE THE AUTHOR TO BRING SERVICE-DRIVEN PASSION AND PURPOSE TO YOUR NEXT EVENT

The Power of Service

This introductory presentation will energize, motivate, and empower. It emphasizes the power of service as the common thread of meaning in our lives regardless of one's faith or belief system, the power that brings great meaning and joy beyond measure.

The Service-Driven Life: Discover the Joy

In lecture or sermon format, this session focuses on the question "Why Serve?" We discover that within the truly service-driven life is great joy—beyond measure—and we begin to embrace that joy.

Change Your Thinking, Change Your Priorities

This presentation is a primer on how to begin and find your path or service. Motivational and empowering, it's filled with concrete ways to learn how to serve in every part of our lives: home and family, vocation, and neighbor.

For more information about the lecture series or to book an event, go to **theservicedrivenlife**.com.

Join the Movement

SERVICE DRIVEN™ INSTITUTE

BECOME A MEMBER

In a world filled with self-service people all "looking out for #1," we want to be a community of people who want to live differently, who want to live our lives in a way that matters and makes a difference.

Won't you join us?

As a member you will be introduced to wonderful people, inspiring ideas, and thoughtful strategies on how to live a service-driven life. Come along with us on a journey that will change your life.

There is no charge or obligation to join.

Membership includes:

- Access to the members-only Service-Driven Institute blog.

- Our monthly e-newsletter and biweekly inspiration reading from Donald Clinebell.

- Priority access to calendaring of lectures, sermons, seminars, and workshops.

- 20% discount on registration for all Service-Driven Institute seminars and workshops.

Join today at **www.theservicedrivenlife.com**

Also by Donald Clinebell

The Service-Driven^{SM} Life:
Discover Your Path to Meaning,
Power & Joy!

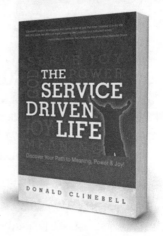

"The only ones among you who will be truly happy are those who will have sought and found how to serve." – Albert Schweitzer

In *The Service-Driven^{SM} Life*, explore how faith sparks service. Written with biblical insight and a Judeo-Christian perspective, this book will provide fresh motivation and excitement to see how your spiritual life can be energized by service even as your life of service is inspired by your faith.

Discover the unshakeable connection between God and service as you spend time in this book. But beware—something might tug at your heart. It may be quite wonderful and unexpected. It may be God moving in your life!

The Service-Driven Life is available at www.theservicedrivenlife.com.